Bits *and* Pieces

18 Small Quilts from Fat Quarters and Scraps

❖

Karen Costello Soltys

D1264841

Martingale® & COMPANY

Bits and Pieces: 18 Small Quilts from
Fat Quarters and Scraps
© 2007 by Karen Costello Soltys

That Patchwork Place® is an imprint of
Martingale & Company®.

Martingale & Company
20205 144th Ave. NE
Woodinville, WA 98072-8478 USA
www.martingale-pub.com

Printed in China
12 11 10 09 08 07   8 7 6 5 4 3 2 1

Credits

President & CEO	Tom Wierzbicki
Publisher	Jane Hamada
Editorial Director	Mary V. Green
Managing Editor	Tina Cook
Technical Editor & Photo Stylist	Ellen Pahl
Copy Editor	Melissa Bryan
Design Director	Stan Green
Illustrator	Robin Strobel
Cover & Text Designer	Patricia Field
Photographers	John Hamel & Brent Kane

Library of Congress Cataloging-in-Publication Data
Library of Congress Control Number: 2007021892

ISBN: 978-1-56477-738-6

Contents

Introduction   5

Basics for Making Little Quilts   6

Squares and Rectangles   13

One Patch Garden   15

Plaid Coins   17

Vintage Bow Ties   21

Box of Chocolates   25

Americana Nine Patch   29

Triangles   33

Waste Not, Want Not   34

Sugarplum Stars   39

Pastel Pinwheels   43

Sunny Lanes   47

Amish-Inspired Shoofly   51

Christmas Goose   55

Diamonds   63

12-Karat Four Patch   65

Antique Diamonds   69

Pennsylvania Star   73

Curves and Circles with Easy Appliqué   79

Japanese Circles   81

Maple Sugar Hearts   85

Sweet Pea   89

Acknowledgments   94

About the Author   95

Introduction

When I took my first quilting class years ago, I never dreamed of where quiltmaking would take me. I had long loved sewing, and took the class on a whim as a way to meet new people upon graduating from college.

Today, many of my closest friends are quilters. Quiltmaking has taken me on a journey from hobby to career, from the East Coast to the West Coast of the United States, and from one who's stitched patterns by dozens of different quilt designers to someone who has created her own collection.

I hope you'll be inspired by this group of small quilts made primarily from fat quarters and scraps. I find them fun and relaxing to make. You can use them for decorating your home (they fit just about anywhere, from a small wall space to a tabletop to draping a cupboard door), and they're perfect for gift giving. They don't take weeks or months to complete, yet your friends and family will recognize the effort and love you've stitched into each one.

This book is divided into chapters based on the type of shape used to make the quilts. I hope you'll consider trying something new, because a small quilt is the perfect opportunity to give a new technique, color scheme, or quilting style a whirl. The time and financial commitment is relatively small and you can practice new skills before moving on to a larger, more time-consuming project.

Long before making the quilts for this book, I was a fan of little projects—not miniatures, but small quilts where the size of the pieces was manageable and the results were pleasing. Quite frankly, little projects like these keep you from getting bored: you don't have to cut too many pieces or watch the same few fabrics feed through your machine endlessly. With perhaps the exception of the hand-appliquéd projects, you can make any of the quilts in this book in a day or two. Machine quilt it and you have a weekend project. Or hand quilt it and you can be done by the next weekend!

Basics for Making Little Quilts

None of the quilts in this book use difficult or out-of-the-ordinary techniques. If you're new to quiltmaking, many of the projects will be easy enough for you to tackle. In this section, I'll share some of the tips I've learned over the years for cutting, piecing, pressing, and finishing quilts. This is by no means an end-all and be-all for quiltmaking. But if you have trouble getting a consistent seam allowance or accurate piecing, you may want to read through the pointers presented here.

Many years ago I learned that successful quilting revolves around three key tasks: cutting accurate pieces, sewing accurately, and pressing accurately. If you have one without the other two, your blocks may end up too large, too small, or off-kilter. When making a little doll quilt or one for a table topper or wall decor, it's not critical that you achieve perfection. But if you want to enhance your quiltmaking sessions, I encourage you to strive for accuracy—sewing is so much more fun when you aren't frustrated by having to rip out a seam or struggle with seams that don't align neatly.

Rotary Cutting Tips

Whenever I take or teach a quilting class, I'm always amazed that there's at least one student who seems to make fabric cutting harder than it has to be. Here are my tips for easy, safe, and accurate cutting.

Safety

- Cut away from yourself—always!

- Always close the blade between cuts to avoid an accident.

- Hold the cutter correctly. Let the cutter rest in the palm of your hand, extend your index finger forward (it will help balance the cutter when you use it), and wrap your other three fingers around the opposite side of the handle from your thumb.

Accuracy

- Always press the fabric before you cut. Fabric with creases will mean quilt patches that have creases. When the creases are pressed out, the patch will be larger than intended.

- Fold the fabric as few times as possible. That means use the largest mat your table can accommodate and then take advantage of its size. If your mat can fit 42"-wide fabric folded just once, leave it folded just once. The more folds you make, the greater chance that your strips will end up looking like the one shown below. Since most of the fabrics used for the projects in this book are fat quarters, I recommend not folding the fabric at all, but cutting a single layer.

Crooked folding leads to crooked strips.

- Don't cut more than four layers at a time. When cutting stacks of squares, triangles, or other shapes, it's tempting to make quick work of the task by stacking up lots of pieces and cutting them all at once. But the more you stack, the less accurate your cutting becomes. The rotary cutter is sharp and can cut through eight layers at a time, but it's difficult to hold a ruler steady on top of a tall stack of 3" squares. If the ruler moves, your squares are no longer square.

- When cutting squares in half to make triangles, position your index finger on the ruler right over the spot where you'll be cutting the triangle points. That way, your ruler will be less likely to slip and give you one set of triangles that's larger than the other.

❖ Use the lines on your ruler—not the ones on the mat—for measuring. Cutting mats are less accurate than rulers. Also, as you cut on the same measurement line over and over, you begin to wear a groove in the mat. Still think it's accurate? What I do is turn my mat over to the plain side, where there are no markings at all to confuse the issue. Then you can lay your fabric any which way on the mat to cut it. You don't end up cutting a groove into the mat and having to throw it away. You can take advantage of every inch of your mat that way.

❖ Use a ruler that has all the markings you'll need. My favorite all-purpose ruler is a 6" x 24" Omnigrid ruler. It has ⅛" increments in both directions; there are dark markings as well as bright markings, so it's easy to see them against both dark and light fabrics; and it has 30°, 45°, and 60° lines, which are great for cutting diamonds and triangles without templates.

❖ When subcutting units from strip sets, first square up the end of the strip set (trim off the end perpendicularly to the strip set), and then line up one of the horizontal inch markings along the strip-set seam line to make sure your units stay true and square. With long strip sets, it's easy to get off-kilter.

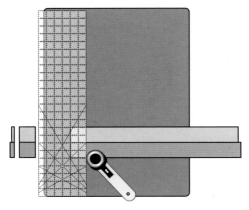

Align horizontal line on ruler
with seam line of strip set.

Piecing Tips

Most of the quilts in this book are fairly easy; none require set-in seams or tricky piecing. But even when sewing squares together, you'll get better results if you sew with a perfect ¼" seam allowance.

Many machines come with a ¼" presser foot or a ¼" guideline on the soleplate. Rather than trusting that it's accurate, sew a test seam to be sure. That way, if you need to adjust the width of your seams, you can mark a stitching guideline on the machine bed with masking tape.

❖ To test your seam allowance, cut two rectangles, 2" x 4". Sew them together along the 4" edge, using a ¼" seam allowance. Press the stitched seam, and then press the seam allowances to one side. Measure the width of the finished piece. It should be 3½" wide. If you cut the pieces accurately yet the patchwork is wider than 3½", you'll need to take a slightly wider seam allowance to compensate. If the patchwork is narrower than 3½", take a slightly narrower seam allowance. Stitch a new test before moving on to your quilt.

❖ When piecing triangle squares, be sure to trim the dog-ears from your pieces (cut perpendicularly to the unsewn edges) before pressing the units open. If you forget, at least trim them off before sewing the triangle square into your quilt block. It reduces bulk, which is important when it's time to actually quilt your quilt, and makes it easier to sew accurate seam intersections when assembling units into a block.

Trim dog-ear
corners.

Pressing Tips

Over the years, I've found that quilters generally take great care with cutting and piecing, but don't give much thought to pressing. Usually the only topic that arises is whether or not to use steam. (Personally, I always use steam, but if you prefer not to, that's perfectly fine, too.)

Good pressing can really improve the quality of your finished quilt blocks. Take a few extra seconds to incorporate these tips, and you'll be glad you did.

* After stitching the seams, take the pieces to your ironing board and press the patchwork just as it came out of your sewing machine—with right sides still together. This will set the seam, making the stitching nice and flat so that the thread takes up less bulk once you press the piece open.

* With the darker patch on top, use the tip of your iron to open up the patchwork and press the seam flat from the right side. This way, the seam allowance will automatically be going toward the dark fabric.

* For long seams, such as those on strip sets or when attaching borders, don't be tempted to slide the iron along the seam allowance. After setting the seam, open up the pieces and, starting in the middle rather than at one end, use the tip of your iron to gently guide the seam open. Then press down on the seam, lift the iron, move to the next spot, and repeat. If you glide the iron along the strip sets, it's easy to stretch them out of shape, creating curved or bowed seams.

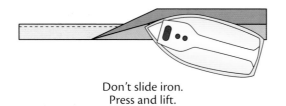

Don't slide iron.
Press and lift.

Assembling a Quilt Top

Take care to use the same accuracy and attention to sewing and pressing when assembling the blocks as you used when making them.

* When stitching rows together, always pin the rows at the seam intersections to make sure you'll have a good match.

* For tricky seam intersections, such as where eight seams come together in a Pinwheel block, you may want to try machine basting the seam first. After basting, open up the rows and check for accuracy. If the points all look good, go back and stitch. If you need to adjust, it's much easier to take out basting stitches than short machine stitches.

* When adding borders, always measure the length or width of the quilt top and trim the borders to fit. This way, the quilt top will be true or square at all the corners. If you simply sew longer strips to the quilt and trim them off after stitching, each side of the quilt may have a border of a slightly different length—which means it won't be square or hang nicely on the wall.

Layering, Basting, and Quilting

Many of the projects in this book were hand quilted, but some were quilted by machine. Deciding up front how and what you want to quilt will help you determine what type of basting to do. Basting with a needle and thread is best for hand quilting, as your quilting thread won't get tangled while you stitch the way it can with safety-pin basting. Conversely, pins are great for machine quilting, because you can easily open and remove them as you approach them.

1. Cut the quilt backing and batting 2" larger than the quilt top. For these small quilts, 1" extra on each side of the quilt top gives plenty of insurance.

2. Press the quilt backing and lay it out on your cutting table with the wrong side facing up. (See tip box below.) Then smooth the batting on top. Finally, center the quilt top on the batting, smoothing out any wrinkles.

3. For thread basting, use a large needle and white thread (it won't show through or bleed through later in case it breaks off and a piece is left between the layers). Use a long running stitch and sew through the layers in horizontal and vertical lines spaced 2" or 3" apart. Try to avoid stitching in areas where you know you'll be quilting, such as ¼" from a seam line.

For pin basting, insert safety pins about 2" or 3" apart in rows. When closing the pins, take care not to move the quilt and bunch up the backing.

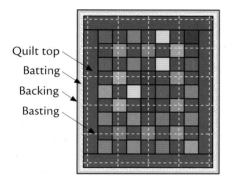

Quilt top
Batting
Backing
Basting

Thread basting

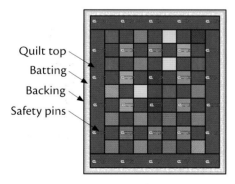

Quilt top
Batting
Backing
Safety pins

Pin basting

4. When basting is complete, quilt as desired! In this book, I've described how each quilt was quilted, whether by hand or machine, as well as what type of pattern was used. I often use masking tape (¼" or wider) to mark stitching lines. If you like to quilt intricate patterns, you may want to mark them on the quilt top before basting your quilt, although it's not impossible to use a stencil to mark a quilt that has already been basted.

Binding

I almost always cut binding strips 2" wide. When folded in half, they become 1" wide, just wide enough to stitch to the quilt with a ¼" seam allowance while still leaving enough to wrap over the quilt edges and provide a ¼" of binding showing on each side of the quilt. Many of my quilting friends like to use wider binding, and I say, "to each her own." However, the quilts in this book are so small that a wider binding might look a little out of proportion. And another thing to keep in mind is that we're working with fat quarters, and cutting wider binding strips may take more fabric than you have on hand.

Before attaching binding to your quilt, use a rotary cutter and long ruler to trim the batting and backing so they are even with the edges of the quilt top. Check the corners of the quilt to make sure they are square. (A larger square ruler is good for this purpose.) Trim the corners if necessary to square them. Also remove any basting threads or pins that weren't removed during the quilting process.

1. Overlap the binding strips, right sides together, at a 90° angle. Sew the strips together, stitching from one intersection point to the other.

Stand Up to Baste

I find standing up to baste is much easier on the back than crawling around on the floor. These quilts are small enough to fit on a cutting mat, so you can baste standing up at your cutting table. Your cutting mat will protect the surface from either needle or safety-pin gouges.

2. Trim the excess fabric, leaving a ¼" seam allowance. Press the seam allowance open.

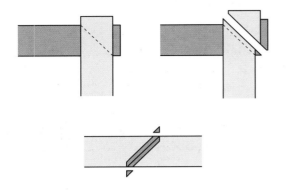

3. Fold the strips in half lengthwise, with wrong sides together. Press.

4. Begin stitching the binding to the quilt along one side, not at a corner. Match the raw edge of the binding with the raw edge of the quilt. Leaving about a 6" tail of binding, start sewing using a ¼" seam allowance.

5. Stop sewing ¼" from the corner; backstitch and remove the quilt from the machine.

6. Turn the quilt so you will be ready to sew the next edge. First, fold the binding so that it is straight up in line with the edge you will now be sewing. Then fold it down and align it with the edge that you will be sewing. The fold should be aligned with the corner of the quilt top.

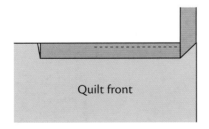

Quilt front

Fold.

7. Sew the binding to the next side of the quilt in the same fashion, stopping ¼" from the corner. Fold the next miter and continue, stitching each side and mitering the corners as you go.

8. Stop stitching about 6" from the point where you started attaching the binding and backstitch. Remove the quilt from the machine.

9. Overlap the beginning and ending tails of the binding. Mark the overlap by the same distance as your binding strips are wide. For instance, if you are using 2"-wide binding, as called for in this book, mark a 2" overlap. (If you're using 2½"-wide strips, the overlap should be 2½".) Trim each end of the binding at the marked points.

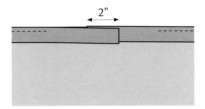

Overlap ends by 2".

10. Open the folds of the two ends of the binding and overlap the ends at right angles, right sides together as shown. Pin the ends together and draw the seam line diagonally between the points where the strips intersect.

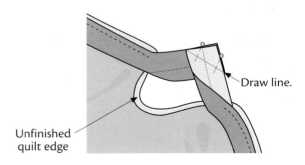

Draw line.

Unfinished quilt edge

11. Sew the binding ends together along the drawn line. Trim the excess fabric, leaving a ¼" seam allowance. Finger-press the seam open, then refold the binding strip and sew it in place on the quilt.

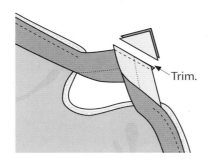

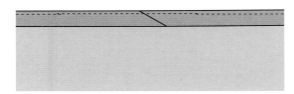

Complete stitching.

12. Fold the binding to the back of the quilt so that it covers the machine stitching. Hand stitch in place, folding the miters as you reach each corner. Take a few stitches to hold the miters in place on both the back and front of the quilt.

Hanging Your Quilt

If you want to hang your quilt, add a hanging sleeve after the binding is applied. Use the same fabric that you used for the backing or use leftover fabric from another project.

1. Measure the width of your quilt. Cut a piece of fabric to that length and a width of 7".

2. Fold the short ends over to the wrong side about ¼"; fold again and then stitch the folds to create a hem on each end.

3. Fold the fabric in half lengthwise, *wrong* sides together, and stitch the raw edges together using a ½" seam. Press the seam allowance open and press the sleeve so that the seam is centered on one side.

4. Position the sleeve on the back of the quilt so that the seam is centered along the underside. Pin the sleeve to the back of the quilt, just below the binding edge. Whipstitch both the top and the bottom of the sleeve to the quilt, being careful that your stitches do not go through to the front of the quilt.

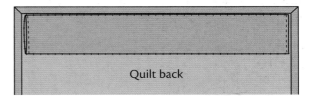

Quilt back

Squares and Rectangles

The quickest and easiest shapes to cut with a rotary cutter are strips, squares, and rectangles. These shapes are also simple to work with, as the seam intersections are easy to match, making for fun projects no matter what your skill level.

You might be surprised to find some quilts in this chapter that look like they're made with triangles. While the finished projects do contain little triangles, all the patchwork starts simply with squares, rectangles, or strips. The triangles are formed when small squares are sewn to other pieces along the diagonal and then pressed open. If you've never used this shortcut technique, I encourage you to try it, especially when working with small pieces. The results are accurate, and up-front cutting time is considerably shortened.

One Patch Garden

Just prior to a move across the country, I got together with my East Coast friends for one last quilting retreat. During that weekend, one of my friends was making a colorful Nine Patch quilt, and another of my friends was snatching the odds and ends of her strip sets out of the scrap basket and piecing them into this darling little One Patch quilt that they surprised me with as a going-away gift. I love how the bright pink, turquoise, orange, blue, and purple squares look like colorful blossoms against the olive green background. Reminds me of a flower garden—one that doesn't require watering or weeding!

Quilt Size: 14" x 17"

Materials

- 1 fat quarter of olive green solid for patchwork and border
- Scraps of hot pink, turquoise, orange, blue, lavender, yellow, and mauve solids for patchwork
- 1 fat eighth of dark olive green for binding
- 1 fat quarter of backing fabric
- 16" x 19" piece of batting

Cutting

From the olive green solid, cut:

- 4 strips, 2" x 21"; crosscut into 31 squares, 2" x 2"
- 4 border strips, 2" x 21"

From the assorted scraps, cut a total of:

- 32 squares, 2" x 2"

From the dark olive green, cut:

- 4 binding strips, 2" x 21"

Assembling the Quilt Top

1. On your design wall, lay out the squares in nine rows of seven squares each. Alternate the squares of assorted colors with the olive green squares, starting with the color squares in the outer corners of the quilt layout.

2. When you are satisfied with the color placement, sew the squares together into rows. Press the seam allowances to one side, alternating the direction from one row to the next.

3. Sew the rows together and press the seam allowances in one direction.

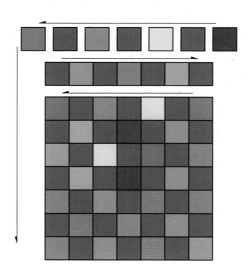

Machine pieced by Karen Bolesta and
Nancy Johnson-Srebro; hand quilted by author.

4. Measure the width of the quilt top through the
center; it should be 11". Trim two of the 2"-wide
olive green border strips to this measurement and
then sew them to the top and bottom of the quilt.
Press the seam allowances toward the borders.

5. Measure the length of the quilt; it should be
17". Trim the remaining two border strips to this
length and sew them to the sides of the quilt top.
Press the seam allowances toward the borders.

Finishing the Quilt

1. Mark any quilting designs on the quilt top
if desired.

2. Place the backing right side down on a table
or floor, and lay the batting on top, smoothing
out any wrinkles. Then add the pressed quilt
top, right side up, on top. Hand or pin baste the
layers together.

3. Quilt by hand or machine. The quilt shown
was hand quilted in a diagonal grid pattern
through the center of each square. The border was
quilted in a freeform (not marked) undulating
vine with leaves to carry out the garden theme.

4. Using the 2"-wide dark olive green strips,
make and attach binding, referring to page 9
as needed.

5. If you want to hang your quilt, add a hanging
sleeve as described on page 11.

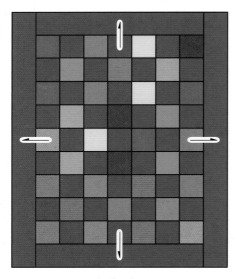

Quilt plan

Plaid Coins

Chinese Coins is a favorite old pattern that combines narrow bits of scrap fabrics into long strips. Here, the coins are all made using strips of plaid fabrics. I was making a large Schoolhouse quilt using plaid fabrics, and simply cut an extra strip from each fabric to use in this little project. All the strips are cut 1½" wide, so dig into your scrap bag to use up leftovers, or start with a group of fabrics you like and cut new strips.

Quilt Size: 21½" x 21½"

Materials

- ½ yard of black dot fabric for sashing, border, and binding
- Plaid scraps or fat eighths★
- ¾ yard of backing fabric
- 24" x 24" piece of batting

   ★*I used 33 different scrap fabrics, but you can use fewer.*

Cutting

From the plaid scraps, cut:
- 60 pieces, 1½" x 4½"

From the black fabric, cut:
- 6 strips, 1½" x 42"; crosscut into:
   - 2 strips, 1½" x 21½"
   - 5 strips, 1½" x 19½"
   - 16 pieces, 1½" x 4½"
- 3 strips, 2" x 42"

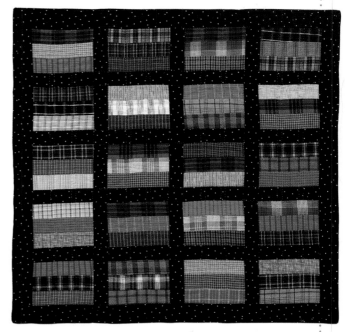

Machine pieced and hand quilted by author.

Assembling the Quilt Top

1. Lay out the plaid pieces in groups of three, separated by the short black pieces. You'll need 15 plaid pieces and 4 black dot pieces for each of the four vertical strips. Rearrange the pieces until you are satisfied with the color placement.

2. Sew the pieces together into vertical strips. Press all seam allowances in one direction.

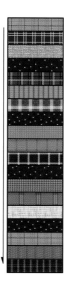

3. Sew a 19½" black strip to the right edge of each plaid strip. Then sew the sections together. Add the remaining 19½" black strip to the left edge of the quilt top. Press all seam allowances toward the black strips.

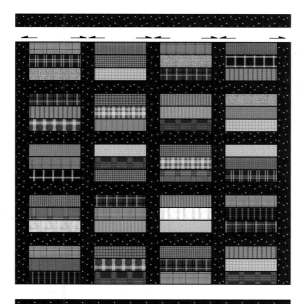

4. Join the 21½" black strips to the top and bottom of the quilt top. Press seams toward the black borders.

Finishing the Quilt

1. If desired, mark any quilting designs on the quilt top.

2. Place the backing right side down on a table or floor, and lay the batting on top, smoothing out any wrinkles. Then add the pressed quilt top, right side up, on top. Hand or pin baste the layers together.

3. Quilt by hand or machine. The quilt shown was hand quilted in the ditch along all the black sashing and border pieces. In addition, I quilted two sets of vertical lines through each column of plaid fabrics by stitching on either side of ¼"-wide masking tape.

4. Using the 2"-wide black strips, make and attach binding, referring to page 9 as needed.

5. If you want to hang your quilt, add a hanging sleeve as described on page 11.

Vintage Bow Ties

My friend Beth owns the most darling little antique doll quilt, made with red-and-black polka-dot bow ties and aqua squares. I just love that well-worn quilt and its perky color scheme. Even though we have many more fabrics available to us today than in past generations, I couldn't seem to find a red-and-black polka-dot fabric. Polka dots are available in just about every colorway imaginable, but I had to settle for red-and-white for my quilt. If red's not your thing, believe me, you can find dozens of other possibilities!

Quilt Size: 15½" x 18½"
Block Size: 3" x 3"

Materials

- 1 fat quarter of red polka-dot fabric for bow ties
- 1 fat quarter of white shirting stripe for bow tie backgrounds
- 1 fat quarter of turquoise print for alternate blocks and binding
- 1 fat quarter of backing fabric
- 18" x 21" piece of batting

Cutting

From the red polka-dot fabric, cut:

- 4 strips, 2" x 21"; crosscut into 30 squares, 2" x 2"
- 2 strips, 1" x 21"; crosscut into 30 squares, 1¼" x 1¼"

From the striped white fabric, cut:

- 4 strips, 2" x 21"; crosscut into 30 squares, 2" x 2"

From the turquoise print, cut:*

- 3 strips, 3½" x 18"; crosscut into 15 squares, 3½" x 3½"
- 4 binding strips, 2" x 18"

  To ensure that you'll have enough fabric, be sure to cut strips along the 18" width of the fat quarter rather than along the 21" length.

Making the Bow Tie Blocks

1. Position a 1" red square on the upper–right corner of each 2" white square, right sides together. If you are using a striped fabric as I did, position the stripes vertically for each unit if you want all the stripes to face the same way in the finished blocks.

Stitch from corner to corner as shown. Press to set the seam, then flip open the red triangle and press again. Trim away the underneath layers to create a ¼" seam allowance and reduce bulk. Make 30.

Make 30.

2. Sew the units from step 1 to the 2" red squares as shown. Press seam the allowances toward the red squares. Sew the units together to make a Bow Tie block. Make 15.

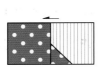

Make 30.

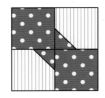

Bowtie block.
Make 15.

Machine pieced and hand quilted by author.

Assembling the Quilt Top

1. Lay out the Bow Tie blocks and the turquoise squares in rows. Notice that the layout isn't exactly symmetrical in the quilt shown. While the blocks and turquoise squares alternate, the top row has

Sew Easy

Because the red squares are so small, it's pretty easy to simply "eyeball" the diagonal line for stitching. However, if you prefer, you can mark the diagonal line from corner to corner on the wrong side using a pencil and ruler. Or, you can fold the squares in half diagonally and crease them to mark the sewing line.

bow ties in the corners but the bottom row has turquoise squares in the corners.

Quilt plan

2. Sew the blocks together into rows, pressing seam allowances toward the turquoise squares. Then sew the rows together. Press all seam allowances in one direction.

Finishing the Quilt

1. If desired, mark any quilting designs on the quilt top.

2. Place the backing right side down on a table or floor, and lay the batting on top, smoothing out any wrinkles. Then add the pressed quilt top, right side up, on top. Hand or pin baste the layers together.

3. Quilt by hand or machine. The quilt shown was hand quilted in the same manner as the original antique quilt that served as my inspiration. The bow ties and white background pieces feature outline quilting, with stitching ¼" from the seams. Each turquoise square was quilted first with an X from corner to corner, and then an on-point square was added. To mark the square, simply place a strip of masking tape from the seams on one bow tie to the seam on the bow tie touching the adjacent side of the turquoise square. When the tape is removed, so are your markings.

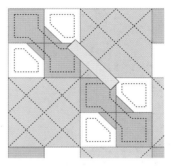

4. Using the 2"-wide turquoise strips, make and attach binding, referring to page 9 as needed.

5. If you want to hang your quilt, add a hanging sleeve as described on page 11.

Box of Chocolates

Square-in-a-square quilts are very popular with quilters of all skill levels. They're easy to make and give you an opportunity to showcase special fabrics if your blocks are large. For this petite version, I wanted to make the patchwork a little more interesting, so instead of using the same fabric on all sides of the center squares, I used two different fabrics per block, placing them in opposite corners to create an interesting zigzag effect. By using a fat-eighth collection of rich browns and soft pinks and creams, the result reminded me of a fancy box of chocolate butter-creams, decorated with pink frosting.

Quilt Size: 16½" x 20½"
Block Size: 4" x 4"

Materials

- 1 fat eighth *each* or scraps of 3 cream prints for patchwork
- 1 fat eighth *each* or scraps of 3 pink prints for patchwork
- 1 fat eighth *each* or scraps of 4 brown prints for patchwork and binding
- ⅝ yard of backing fabric★
- 19" x 23" piece of batting
- 20 buttons, approximately ½" to ⅝" in diameter

  ★*You can use ⅜ yard if you don't mind a seam in your quilt back.*

Cutting

From *each* of the pink prints, cut:
- 2 strips, 1½" x 21" (6 total)
- 2 strips, 2½" x 21" (6 total)

From *3* of the brown prints, cut:
- 2 strips, 1½" x 21" (6 total)
- 2 strips, 2½" x 21" (6 total)

From *each* of the cream prints, cut:
- 7 squares, 2½" x 2½" (21 total; 1 will be extra)

From the remaining brown print, cut:
- 4 binding strips, 2" x 21"

Making the Blocks

1. Pair a 1½"-wide pink strip with a 1½"-wide brown strip. Sew them together along the long edges. Press the seam allowance toward the brown fabric. Repeat to make a total of six strip sets, pairing the 1½" strips of the same pink and brown fabrics together. Cut the strip sets into 1½"-wide segments (40 total); you'll need 20 matching pairs of segments.

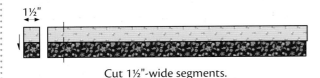

Cut 1½"-wide segments.

2. Sew the 2½"-wide pink and brown strips together in the same manner, again pairing the same fabric combinations. Cut the strip sets into 1½"-wide segments (40 total); you'll need 20 matching pairs of segments.

Cut 1½"-wide segments.

3. For each block, select one cream square and two matching segments from step 1. Sew the segments to opposite sides of the cream square, making sure that the pink squares are diagonally opposite from one another, not directly across. Press the seam allowances toward the segments. Make 20.

Make 20.

4. Sew matching segments from step 2 to each partial block as shown, placing the pink pieces next to the previously attached pink squares. Press both seam allowances in the same direction for ease of matching seams when assembling the quilt top. Make 20 blocks.

Make 20.

Assembling the Quilt Top

1. Lay out the blocks in five horizontal rows of four blocks each. Make sure that the pink fabrics are in the upper-left and lower-right corners of all blocks in order to create the diagonal pattern.

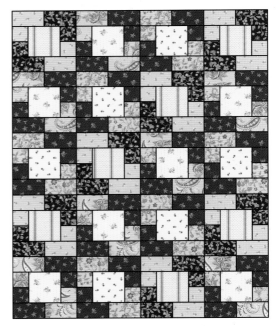

Quilt plan

Machine pieced and machine quilted by author.

2. When you are satisfied with the placement of colors and fabrics, sew the blocks together into rows. If necessary, rotate the blocks 180° so that adjoining seam allowances are pressed in opposite directions for easier seam alignment.

3. Sew the rows together and press seam allowances in one direction.

Finishing the Quilt

1. If desired, mark any quilting designs on the quilt top.

2. If necessary, piece the quilt backing and press the seam allowance to one side. Place the backing right side down on a table or floor, and lay the batting on top, smoothing out any wrinkles. Then add the pressed quilt top, right side up, on top. Hand or pin baste the layers together.

3. Quilt by hand or machine. The quilt shown was machine quilted with continuous curved lines. Rather than mark the quilt, I simply stitched from one corner of a brown section to the opposite corner, bowing the stitching line to take advantage of the L shape of the fabric pieces. You can quilt along one brown diagonal, turn your quilt a quarter turn, and continue stitching along the pink diagonal for easy no-mark quilting with very little starting and stopping. The numbers in the diagram merely show where to start and the first several turns. You can continue stitching beyond turn eight without stopping.

No-mark quilting pattern

4. Using the 2"-wide brown strips, make and attach binding, referring to page 9 as needed.

5. Sew a button in the center of each light print square, sewing through all layers to secure it.

6. If you want to hang your quilt, add a hanging sleeve as described on page 11.

Americana Nine Patch

Snowball and Nine Patch quilts are a familiar sight to most quilters. Even young girls learning how to sew in days gone by often made doll quilts featuring this design. While the pattern is basic, it's easy to vary the look of the quilt simply by altering the color placement within the Nine Patches or the Snowball blocks. Here, I chose to make a chain of dark blue along one diagonal and lighter blue along the other. And by using the same background color for both types of blocks, it makes it hard to tell where one block stops and the next block starts. You can follow my color scheme, or devise your own plan by varying the value placement.

Quilt Size: 21½" x 21½"
Block Size: 3" x 3"

Materials

- ⅜ yard of light print for blocks
- 1 fat quarter of red print for Nine Patch blocks and border
- 1 fat quarter *each* of medium blue and dark blue print for blocks
- 1 fat quarter of medium-dark blue print for binding
- ¾ yard of backing fabric
- 24" x 24" piece of batting

Cutting

From *each* of the medium and dark blue prints, cut:

- 3 strips, 1½" x 21" (6 total)
- 24 squares, 1½" x 1½" (48 total)

From the light print, cut:

- 2 strips, 3½" x 42"; crosscut into 12 squares, 3½" x 3½"
- 4 strips, 1½" x 42"; cut strips in half to yield 8 strips, 1½" x 21" (1 will be extra)

From the red print, cut:

- 2 strips, 1½" x 21"
- 4 strips, 3½" x 15½"

From the medium-dark blue print, cut:

- 5 binding strips, 2" x 21"

Making the Nine Patch Blocks

1. Join one dark blue, one light print, and one medium blue strip along their long edges as shown. Press the seam allowances toward the blue strips. Repeat to make three of these strip sets. From the strip sets, cut 34 segments, 1½" wide.

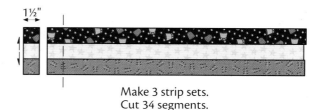

1½"

Make 3 strip sets.
Cut 34 segments.

Machine pieced and hand quilted by author.

Making the Snowball Blocks

1. Mark a diagonal line from corner to corner on the wrong side of the medium blue and dark blue 1½" squares. Then position a medium blue square on diagonally opposite corners of a 3½" light square, right sides together. Sew along the marked lines and trim away the corner fabric, leaving a ¼" seam allowance. Press the resulting blue triangles open. Make 12 of these units.

Make 12.

2. Repeat step 1, sewing the dark blue squares to the remaining two corners of each block to complete 12 Snowball blocks.

Make 12.

2. In the same manner, make a strip set using two light strips and one 1½" x 21" red print strip. Press the seam allowances toward the red print. Repeat to make two strip sets. From these strip sets, cut 17 segments, 1½" wide.

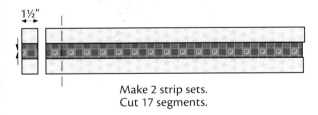

Make 2 strip sets.
Cut 17 segments.

3. Arrange the segments from steps 1 and 2 into Nine Patch blocks. You'll need two segments with blue squares and one with a red square for each block. Be sure to rotate the blue segments as shown so that the medium blue squares are diagonally opposite one another. Sew the segments together and press the seam allowances toward the blue segments. Make a total of 17 blocks.

Assembling the Quilt Top

1. Lay out 13 of the Nine Patch blocks and the 12 Snowball blocks in five rows of five blocks each. Start with a Nine Patch block in the outer corners, and alternate with the Snowball blocks. Position the blocks so that the Nine Patch blocks all have medium blue squares in the upper-left corner. The Snowball blocks should have dark blue triangles in the upper-left corner. This way, the medium blue and dark blue patches will be adjacent, forming a secondary pattern when the blocks are stitched together.

Make 17.

2. Sew the blocks together into rows, pressing the seam allowances toward the Nine Patch blocks. Then sew the rows together and press the seam allowances all in one direction.

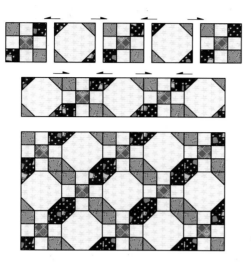

3. Sew a red print border strip to the left and right sides of the quilt top. Press the seam allowances toward the border.

4. Sew the remaining Nine Patch blocks to the two remaining red print border strips. To continue the design, make sure that the medium blue squares are in the upper left, as shown, for both borders. Press the seam allowances toward the red strips, and then sew the borders to the top and bottom of the quilt top, matching the seam intersections. Press.

Finishing the Quilt

1. If desired, mark any quilting designs on the quilt top.

2. Place the backing right side down on a table or floor, and lay the batting on top, smoothing out any wrinkles. Then add the pressed quilt top, right side up, on top. Hand or pin baste the layers together.

3. Quilt by hand or machine. The quilt shown was hand quilted, first with straight lines creating an X in each Nine Patch, then with curved lines in each Snowball block emphasizing the diagonal movement of the design. The quilting extends from the Snowball blocks into the light fabric of the Nine Patches to blur the lines between the blocks. The border is quilted in a diagonal cross-hatch pattern.

4. Using the 2"-wide medium-dark blue strips, make and attach binding, referring to page 9 as needed.

5. If you want to hang your quilt, add a hanging sleeve as described on page 11.

Triangles

While strips and squares are easy, most quilters find that triangles are among the most versatile shapes in traditional patchwork quilts. They can be stitched together to make pieced squares (I call them triangle squares), or combined with other shapes to make everything from basket feet to dogtooth borders.

Literally hundreds of patchwork blocks are at least partially composed of triangles of one sort or another. So why do they remain the bane of some quilters? My take is that some quilters just feel triangles will be harder to work with because of a bias edge (the edge that's cut diagonally across the fabric grain). If you take care not to handle cut triangles too much before they're sewn into your block, I promise, they really don't need to be feared. Mastering working with triangles will open up a world of patchwork possibilities for you.

Waste Not, Want Not

These two little quilts came to be when my quilt group decided to make a twin-size mystery quilt. I chose the white print fabric for my quilt's background, and a variety of fat quarters in shades of red, blue, green, purple, and gold for the blocks. I didn't realize, at the time, that we'd be making extra-large flying-geese units and trimming off rather large triangles from the corners of these units. Not wanting to toss so many triangles in the trash or my overflowing scrap basket, I carefully trimmed the flying-geese corners and sewed the pairs of triangles together. I had enough to make both of the quilts shown here, and still had a few leftovers! You can easily make either or both of these quilts from scratch.

Quilt Sizes:
Flags: 16¼" x 20¾"
Barn Raising: 22½" x 22½"
Block Size: 2¼" x 2¼"

Materials

- ⅝ yard of white print for triangles (enough for both quilts)
- ⅝ yard total of assorted red, blue, gold, purple, and green scraps for triangles
- ¼ yard of blue print for border (Barn Raising quilt only)
- 1 fat quarter of binding fabric for each quilt
- ½ yard of backing fabric for Flags quilt
- ⅔ yard of backing fabric for Barn Raising quilt
- 19" x 23" piece of batting for Flags quilt
- 25" x 25" piece of batting for Barn Raising quilt

Cutting

From the white print, cut:
- 64 squares, 3⅛" x 3⅛" (This is enough for both quilts; to make just one, cut 32 squares.)

From the assorted scraps, cut:
- 64 squares, 3⅛" x 3⅛" (This is enough for both quilts; to make just one, cut 32 squares.)

From the blue print (for Barn Raising quilt), cut:
- 3 border strips, 2½" x 42"

From the binding fabric, cut:
- 5 strips, 2" x 21" (enough for 1 quilt)

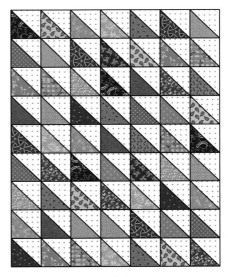

Flags quilt (left) and Barn Raising quilt (right); machine pieced and machine quilted by author.

Making the Triangle Squares

1. Draw a diagonal line from corner to corner on the wrong side of the white squares.

2. Layer a white square with a colored square, right sides together. Stitch ¼" from each side of the marked line. Repeat for all squares. Cut the squares apart on the drawn line and press the resulting triangle squares with the seam allowance toward the dark fabric. Make 63 for the Flags quilt and 64 for the Barn Raising quilt.

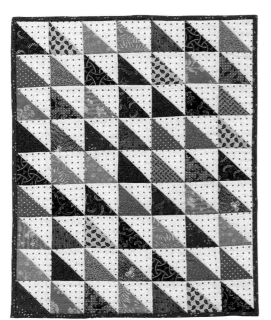

Mark. Stitch. Cut.

Press.

Assembling the Quilt Tops

1. For the Flags quilt, lay out 63 triangle squares in nine rows of seven squares each. Make sure all dark triangles are pointing in the same direction as shown. Sew the squares together into rows; press the seam allowances in the opposite direction from row to row. Sew the rows together, taking care to match the points as you pin the seams together. Press the seam allowances in one direction.

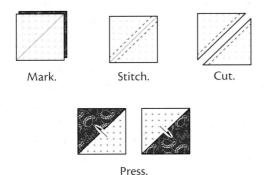

Flag quilt layout

2. For the Barn Raising quilt, lay out 64 triangle squares in eight rows of eight squares each. Each quadrant of this quilt top will contain 16 squares; for each quadrant, make sure the dark triangles point toward the center of the quilt as shown.

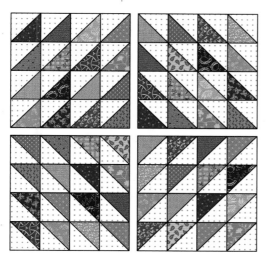

Barn Raising quilt layout

3. Sew the squares together into rows, pressing the seams in the opposite direction from row to row. Sew the rows together and press the seam allowances in one direction.

4. Measure the width of the quilt top. It should be 18½". Cut one of the 2½" border strips into two strips this length and sew them to the top and bottom of the quilt. Press the seam allowances toward the borders.

Easy Antiquing

For a crinkled, vintage look, I machine washed and dried the quilts after adding the binding. Because I'd pre-washed the fabrics but not the 100%-cotton batting, the batting shrank during washing, creating that timeworn look.

---

5. For the side borders, measure the length of the quilt top. It should be 22½". Cut the remaining border strips to this length and sew them to the sides of the quilt. Press the seam allowances toward the borders.

Quilt plan

Finishing the Quilts

1. If desired, mark any quilting designs on the quilt tops.

2. Place the backing right side down on a table or floor, and lay the batting on top, smoothing out any wrinkles. Then add the pressed quilt top, right side up, on top. Hand or pin baste the layers together.

3. Quilt by hand or machine. The quilts shown were both machine quilted. The Flag quilt was quilted in the ditch along both the horizontal and vertical seams as well as the diagonal ones. The Barn Raising quilt was free-motion quilted with feather motifs in the center and border.

4. Using the 2"-wide binding strips, make and attach binding, referring to page 9 as needed.

5. If you want to hang your quilts, add a hanging sleeve to each one as described on page 11.

Sugarplum Stars

The Ohio Star block is a perennial favorite among quilters. For a small quilt, I like merging the stars together so that side-by-side stars share the same set of star points. This effect keeps the eye moving across the little quilt top. Another trick to making the quilt interesting is to use a variety of prints, plaids, and stripes for the star centers. Of course, if you don't have a scrap basket piled high with suitable choices, you could easily cut all the purple star centers from the same print as used for the border accent.

Quilt Size: 20½" x 24½"
Unit Size: 2" x 2"

Materials

- ½ yard of small-scale purple print for star points and binding
- 1 fat quarter of tan check for background
- 1 fat quarter of purple print for border accent and star centers
- 1 fat quarter of caramel print for border
- Scraps of 5 additional purple prints, plaids, and stripes for star centers
- ¾ yard of backing fabric★
- 23" x 27" piece of batting

  ★You can use ⅜ yard if you don't mind a seam in your quilt back.

Cutting

From the tan check, cut:

- 16 squares, 3¼" x 3¼"; cut diagonally into quarters to yield 64 triangles (2 will be extra)
- 20 squares, 2½" x 2½"

From the small-scale purple print, cut:

- 16 squares, 3¼" x 3¼"; cut diagonally into quarters to yield 64 triangles (2 will be extra)
- 3 binding strips, 2" x 42"

From the purple accent print, cut:

- 4 strips, 1" x 21"
- 2 squares, 2½" x 2½"

From *each* of the 5 purple scraps, cut:

- 2 squares, 2½" x 2½" (10 total)

From the caramel print, cut:

- 4 border strips, 3½" x 21"

Piecing the Units

The star-point units are made from quarter-square triangles. This allows the finished units to have straight-of-grain edges on the outside of the block, keeping it stable. Unlike half-square triangles, the short edges on these triangles are the bias edges.

1. Sew the tan check triangles to the purple triangles with their short edges aligned and tan triangles on top. Trim the dog-ear corners and then press the units open with the seam allowances toward the purple triangles. Make 62 units, all with the purple triangles on the left.

Make 62.

2. Join pairs of the triangle units, butting the seam intersections. The purple fabric and tan check fabric should be adjoining as you sew. Trim the dog-ears and press the units open. Make 31.

Make 31.

Assembling the Quilt

1. Lay out the units in nine rows of seven units each. In odd-numbered rows (1, 3, 5, 7, and 9), alternate tan check squares and purple-and-tan triangle units; position the triangle units like bow ties, with the purple triangles on the left and right sides of the units.

In the even-numbered rows, alternate the triangle units with the 2½" assorted purple squares. In these rows, position the triangle units with the purple triangles on the top and bottom.

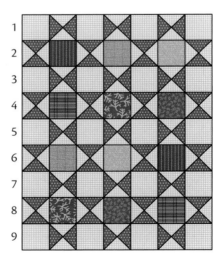

2. Once you are satisfied with the arrangement of the triangle units and purple squares, sew the pieces together into rows. Press the seam allowances toward the tan check and purple squares. Sew the rows together, matching seam allowances. Press the seam allowances in one direction.

Machine pieced and hand quilted by author.

Adding the Border

1. Measure the length of your quilt top; it should measure 18½". Trim two of the caramel border strips and two of the purple accent strips to this length. Fold the purple strips in half lengthwise, *wrong* sides together, and press. Position each purple strip along one edge of a caramel strip and machine baste in place with a narrow (⅛") seam allowance.

2. Reset the stitch length and sew the caramel borders to the sides of the quilt top, making sure to sew the edge with the attached purple accent strip. Press the seam allowances and the purple accent strips toward the borders.

3. Measure the width of the quilt top; it should measure 20½". Trim the remaining two caramel border strips and purple accent strips to this length. Prepare the accent strips as before and then sew the border strips to the top and bottom of the quilt. Again, press the seam allowances and the purple accent strips toward the border.

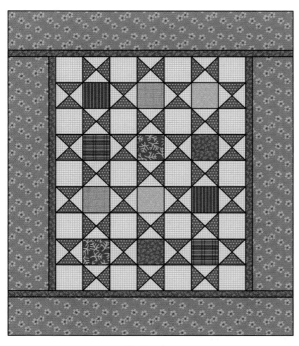

Quilt plan

Keeping the Accent in Line

To keep the purple accent strips from flopping over and covering up the triangle points in the stars, appliqué the loose edge to the caramel border. This technique will give your quilt a narrow strip of accent color and dimension, plus it's easier to do accurately than inserting a very narrow border.

Finishing the Quilt

1. If desired, mark any quilting designs on the quilt top.

2. If necessary, piece the quilt backing and press the seam allowance to one side. Place the backing right side down on a table or floor, and lay the batting on top, smoothing out any wrinkles. Then add the pressed quilt top, right side up, on top. Hand or pin baste the layers together.

3. Quilt by hand or machine. The quilt shown was quilted by hand with Xs through the plain squares and parallel diagonal lines in the border.

4. Using the 2"-wide small-scale purple print strips, make and attach binding, referring to page 9 as needed.

5. If you want to hang your quilt, add a hanging sleeve as described on page 11.

Pastel Pinwheels

A far cry from brightly colored plastic pinwheels enjoyed by children at the beach, the pinwheels in this quilt are stitched from subtle hues. I combined two sets of favorite fabrics—Japanese prints and hand-dyed pastel solids—for a look that could be equally at home in a spare modern environment or one with lots of antiques and vintage furnishings.

Quilt Size: 16½" x 20½"
Block Size: 4" x 4"

Materials

- 1 fat eighth *each* of 10 assorted pastel solids
- 1 fat eighth *each* of 10 assorted light to medium subtle prints
- 1 fat quarter of light striped fabric for binding
- ½ yard of backing fabric
- 19" x 23" piece of batting

Cutting

From each pastel solid, cut:

- 4 squares, 2⅞" x 2⅞" (40 total)

From each light to medium print, cut:

- 4 squares, 2⅞" x 2⅞" (40 total)

From the striped fabric, cut:

- 5 binding strips, 2" x 21"

Making the Blocks

1. Stack all like-colored pastel squares together in groups of four. You should have 10 stacks. Stack the print fabrics together in the same way and then pair each stack with a stack of solid fabrics. Each grouping will yield two blocks for your quilt.

2. To piece the triangles, you can cut all the squares in half diagonally and then sew a print triangle to a solid triangle. Or, you can mark a diagonal line on the wrong side of each pastel square, layer the square right sides together with a print square, and stitch ¼" on each side of the marked line. Then cut the squares apart on the line. You will have 8 matching triangle squares for each combination (80 total).

For either method, trim the dog-ear corners and press the seam allowances to one side. Press the seam allowances toward either the print or solid for all units and blocks. This will make it easier to assemble the pinwheels and join the blocks together later. I pressed toward the solid fabrics because they were more opaque.

 or

Make 8 matching triangle squares.

When Eight Points Come Together

Admittedly, it can be tricky to make nice pinwheel points where eight fabric patches come together at the same spot. For the best results, I like to stick a straight pin through the X of stitching intersections on one row and then through the matching X on the adjoining row. While this pin is still sticking perpendicularly through the two points to be matched, I take another straight pin and pin just before the seam intersection, and then use a third pin just behind the seam intersection. This holds my matching points in place without distorting them, as would happen if I tried to pin exactly through all eight layers of fabric at once.

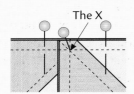
The X

For sewing, stitch a scant $1/4$" seam, making sure your seam line is just shy of the X intersection. Open up the seam and see how it looks. If needed, you can sew the seam again with a slightly wider seam allowance. That's much easier than having to rip out one that's too wide to begin with.

3. Place a set of four matching triangle squares in a four-patch arrangement. Make sure the print fabrics radiate around the center of the block, always rotating in the same direction so that when you assemble the quilt, the print fabrics will always adjoin a solid fabric. Sew the triangle squares together in pairs and then sew the pairs together to complete the block. Make 20 Pinwheel blocks.

Make 20.

Assembling the Quilt Top

1. Lay out the blocks in five rows of four blocks each. Rearrange the blocks as desired until you are pleased with the balance of colors and prints.

2. Sew the blocks together into rows, pressing seam allowances in opposite directions from one row to the next. Then sew the rows together to complete the quilt top.

Quilt layout

Machine pieced and hand quilted by author.

Finishing the Quilt

1. If desired, mark any quilting designs on the quilt top.

2. Place the backing right side down on a table or floor, and lay the batting on top, smoothing out any wrinkles. Then add the pressed quilt top, right side up, on top. Hand or pin baste the layers together.

3. Quilt by hand or machine. The quilt shown was hand quilted by simply stitching in the ditch along all seam lines: vertical, horizontal, and diagonal. For easier quilting in the ditch, be sure to stitch on the side of the seam that doesn't have the seam allowances pressed beneath it.

4. Using the 2"-wide striped strips, make and attach binding, referring to page 9 as needed.

5. If you want to hang your quilt, add a hanging sleeve as described on page 11.

Sunny Lanes

Sunny Lanes is a traditional block made of triangle squares and four-patch units. I've only seen it made from a wide array of scrap fabrics in a much larger scale. I thought it would be fun to make a small version in a limited color palette. But while I chose just three colors, I couldn't use just three fabrics! Why use one double-pink or poison green when you can use three or four of each? The color palette for this project is reminiscent of late-1800s quilts, but the techniques are definitely twenty-first century.

Quilt Size: 20½" x 20½"
Block Size: 8" x 8"

Materials

- 1 fat quarter of white print for background
- 1 fat quarter of dark green print for blocks and border
- 1 fat quarter of medium green print for blocks and binding
- 1 fat eighth *each* or scraps of 2 additional green prints for blocks
- 1 fat eighth *each* or scraps of 4 assorted double-pink prints for blocks
- ¾ yard of backing fabric★
- 23" x 23" piece of batting

  ★*You can use ⅜ yard if you don't mind a seam in your quilt back.*

Cutting

From *each* of the 4 pink prints, cut:

- 2 strips, 1½" x 21"; crosscut into a total of 64 squares (16 from each pink), 1½" x 1½"

From the white print, cut:

- 3 strips, 2⅞" x 21"; crosscut into 16 squares, 2⅞" x 2⅞"
- 5 strips, 1½" x 21"; crosscut into 64 squares, 1½" x 1½"

From the dark green print, cut:

- 4 border strips, 2½" x 21"
- 4 squares, 2⅞" x 2⅞"

From the medium green print, cut:

- 5 binding strips, 2" x 21"
- 4 squares, 2⅞" x 2⅞"

From *each* of the remaining 2 green prints, cut:

- 4 squares, 2⅞" x 2⅞" (8 total)

Making the Blocks

1. Select two matching pink squares and two white squares and arrange them into a four-patch unit as shown. Sew the squares into pairs and press the seam allowances toward the pink squares. Sew the pairs together, matching the seam intersections. Press. Repeat to make a total of 32 four-patch units.

Make 32.

2. To piece the triangles, you can either cut all the white and green squares in half diagonally and then sew a green triangle to a white triangle, or you can mark a diagonal line on the wrong side of each white square, layer the square right sides together with a green square, and stitch ¼" on each side of the marked line. Then cut the squares apart on the line. You will have 32 triangle squares. For either method, trim the dog-ear corners and press the seam allowances to one side.

Make 32.

3. To assemble one block, select eight triangle squares and eight four-patch units. Be sure to mix up the fabrics so your quilt will have an overall, but subtle, scrappy look. Lay out the units in four rows of four units each, making sure to arrange them as shown so that the diagonal path will be apparent.

Machine pieced and hand quilted by author.

Sew the units together into rows, press the seam allowances toward the four patches, and then sew the rows together. Press. Repeat to make four blocks.

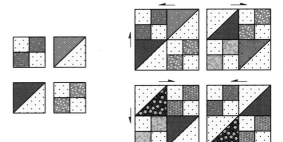

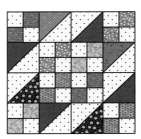

Make 4.

Assembling the Quilt Top

1. Lay out the four blocks as shown, rotating them so that the green-and-white triangle squares form a diamond-shaped pathway around the quilt.

2. Sew the blocks together in pairs and then sew the pairs together, matching all seam intersections. Press.

Quilt layout

3. Measure the length of the quilt top; it should measure 16½". Trim two of the dark green border strips to this length. Sew the borders to opposite sides of the quilt and press the seam allowances toward the borders. Measure the width of the quilt top, including the borders; it should measure 20½". Trim the remaining two border strips to this length. Sew the borders to the top and bottom of the quilt and press.

Finishing the Quilt

1. If desired, mark any quilting designs on the quilt top.

2. If necessary, piece the quilt backing and press the seam allowance to one side. Place the backing right side down on a table or floor, and lay the batting on top, smoothing out any wrinkles. Then add the pressed quilt top, right side up, on top. Hand or pin baste the layers together.

3. Quilt by hand or machine. In the quilt shown, I simply hand quilted ¼" inside all of the green triangles and diagonally through the center of each four-patch unit, using ¼"-wide quilter's masking tape as a guideline. To emphasize the pathways, I stitched the white triangles with parallel diagonal lines. I quilted the border with small tulips that alternate direction.

4. Using the 2"-wide dark green strips, make and attach binding, referring to page 9 as needed.

5. If you want to hang your quilt, add a hanging sleeve as described on page 11.

Amish-Inspired Shoofly

Blue-green, turquoise, aquamarine—whatever you call this color, it's always been one of my favorites. Before the idea for this book was born, I had a little over a half yard of dusty turquoise fabric that I was saving for a special project. It was a hand-dyed fabric and I couldn't get more, so I decided to use every last bit of it for this quilt's border. Since I didn't have enough of any single blue, brown, or aqua, I decided to make an Amish-inspired quilt, following their "make-do" philosophy. I chose Shoofly blocks, not only because they're popular in Amish quiltmaking, but also because shoofly pie is the name of a favorite breakfast treat in my native southeastern Pennsylvania, which is home to Mennonite and Amish communities.

Quilt Size: 23¼" x 29½"
Block Size: 4½" x 4½"

Materials

- ⅝ yard of dusty turquoise solid for outer border
- ⅜ yard of dark cinnamon for inner border and binding
- 1 fat quarter of light cinnamon for Shoofly blocks
- 1 fat quarter of dark blue for Shoofly blocks
- 1 fat quarter of medium blue for setting triangles
- 1 fat eighth of dusty blue for setting squares
- ⅞ yard of backing fabric
- 25" x 32" piece of batting

Cutting

From the light cinnamon, cut:
- 6 squares, 2" x 2"
- 12 squares, 2⅜" x 2⅜"

From the dark blue, cut:
- 24 squares, 2" x 2"
- 12 squares, 2⅜" x 2⅜"

From the dusty blue, cut:
- 2 squares, 5" x 5"

From the medium blue, cut:
- 2 squares, 7¾" x 7¾"; cut diagonally into quarters to yield 8 setting triangles (2 will be extra)
- 2 squares, 4¼" x 4¼"; cut in half diagonally to yield 4 corner triangles

From the dark cinnamon, cut:
- 2 strips, 1½" x 42"
- 3 strips, 2" x 42"

From the dusty turquoise, cut:
- 4 strips, 4½" x 42"

Making the Blocks

1. To piece the triangles, you can cut the 2⅜" light cinnamon and dark blue triangles in half diagonally and then sew a cinnamon triangle to a blue triangle. Or, you can mark a diagonal line on the wrong side of the cinnamon squares, layer the squares right sides together with the blue squares, and stitch ¼" on each side of the marked line. Then cut the squares apart on the drawn line. Make 24 triangle squares. Press the seam allowances toward the dark blue triangles.

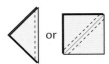 or

Make 24.

2. Lay out one 2" light cinnamon square, four 2" dark blue squares, and four triangle squares from step 1 in a nine-patch arrangement. Sew the pieces together in rows and then sew the rows together to complete a Shoofly block, pressing the seam allowances toward the dark blue fabric. Repeat to make six blocks.

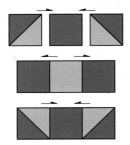 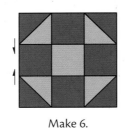

Make 6.

Assembling the Quilt Top

1. Lay out the six Shoofly blocks, the two dusty blue setting squares, and the medium blue side and corner setting triangles in diagonal rows. Sew the blocks, setting squares, and side triangles together into rows, pressing the seam allowances toward the setting squares and triangles.

Machine pieced and machine quilted by author.

2. Sew the rows together, matching seam intersections. Add the corner triangles last and press. The setting triangles were cut a bit oversize for easier cutting and piecing. Trim and square up the quilt top, making sure to leave ¼" beyond the points of all the blocks for seam allowances.

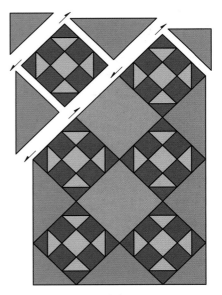

Quilt layout

3. Measure the length of the quilt top; it should measure 19½". Cut two pieces this length from a dark cinnamon border strip. Sew them to the sides of the quilt top and press the seam allowances toward the borders. Measure the width of the quilt top; it should measure 15¼". Cut two pieces from the remaining dark cinnamon border strips and sew them to the top and bottom of the quilt top. Press.

4. Measure, trim, and sew the dusty turquoise borders to the quilt top in the same manner as for the dark cinnamon border.

Quilt plan

Easy Marking

A Hera marker is a white plastic tool available at quilt shops. It is perfect for marking straight lines. It does not leave a mark as a pencil would, but simply creates a crease that you see for stitching. There are no marks to remove afterward.

Finishing the Quilt

1. If desired, mark any quilting designs on the quilt top.

2. Place the backing right side down on a table or floor, and lay the batting on top, smoothing out any wrinkles. Then add the pressed quilt top, right side up, on top. Hand or pin baste the layers together.

3. Quilt by hand or machine. The quilt shown was machine quilted. First, I stitched in the ditch between all blocks and setting pieces, as well as on both sides of the dark cinnamon border to stabilize the quilt. Then I stitched in the ditch around all pieces in each Shoofly block. I added a continuous-line floral design in the plain setting squares and cross-hatching in the outer border. You can mark the cross-hatching with masking tape or by using a Hera marker and your rotary-cutting ruler.

4. Using the 2"-wide dark cinnamon strips, make and attach binding, referring to page 9 as needed.

5. If you want to hang your quilt, add a hanging sleeve as described on page 11.

Christmas Goose

I've always been drawn to patchwork designs that form a diagonal pattern. The Goose Chase block is just one such design, but piecing its many little triangles and setting triangles seemed too tedious with traditional cutting and sewing methods. I turned to foundation piecing to make this quilt quite manageable. You can't beat foundation piecing for accuracy—getting all those little triangles to be perfectly pointy and match up with those in the next block is a breeze. This quilt is just right for topping your dining-room table or adorning a wall during the Christmas season.

Quilt Size: 24½" x 24½"
Block Size: 6" x 6"

Materials

- 1 fat quarter *each* of 5 assorted beiges for background and borders
- 1 fat quarter *each* of 5 assorted dark reds for blocks and pieced border
- 1 fat quarter *each* of 5 assorted dark greens for blocks and pieced border
- 1 fat quarter of dark red for binding
- ⅞ yard of backing fabric
- 27" x 27" piece of batting
- Paper for Foundation Piecing (Martingale & Company)

Cutting

Five of the blocks have red centers and green geese; four have green centers and red geese. In the quilt shown, one red, one green, and one beige fabric are used in each block.

Cutting for Blocks

From the reds, cut:

- 4 sets of 6 matching squares, 3" x 3"; cut in half diagonally to yield 12 triangles per block for the 4 blocks with green centers
- 5 squares, 2" x 2", for the centers of 5 blocks
- 5 squares, 4¾" x 4¾", that match the block centers; cut diagonally into quarters to yield 4 triangles per block (20 total)

From the beiges, cut:

- 9 sets of 10 matching squares, 2¼" x 2¼"; cut in half diagonally once to yield 20 triangles per block (180 total)

From the greens, cut:

- 5 sets of 6 matching squares, 3" x 3"; cut in half diagonally to yield 12 triangles per block for the 5 blocks with red centers
- 4 squares, 2" x 2", for the centers of 4 blocks
- 4 squares, 4¾" x 4¾", that match the block centers; cut diagonally into quarters to yield 4 triangles per block (16 total)

Cutting for Borders and Binding

From *each* of the 5 remaining beige fabrics, cut:

- 1 strip, 1½" x 21" (5 total)

Designed by author. Machine pieced by Shannon Camardo and machine quilted by author.

From the remaining beige scraps, cut:

- 42 squares, 2¼" x 2¼"; cut in half diagonally to yield 84 triangles
- 2½" x 21" strips; crosscut into the following lengths:
  - 1 piece, 5½" long
  - 1 piece, 4½" long
  - 2 pieces, 4" long
  - 3 pieces, 3½" long
  - 6 pieces, 3" long
  - 3 pieces, 2½" long

From the greens, cut:

- 2 squares, 2" x 2"
- 9 squares, 3" x 3"; cut in half diagonally to yield 18 triangles (1 will be extra)

From the reds, cut:

- 2 squares, 2" x 2"
- 9 squares, 3" x 3"; cut in half diagonally to yield 18 triangles (1 will be extra)

From the red for binding, cut:

- 6 strips, 2" x 21"

Piecing the Blocks

Each block is made from just three fabrics: one red, one green, and one beige print. In each block the center square and the largest triangles are the same color, while the smaller triangles that form the X design are the opposite color. All background pieces are beige. For each block select the following: 20 matching beige triangles, 12 matching 3" triangles, and one 2" center square with four matching triangles cut from 4¾" squares.

1. Using the block foundation patterns on page 60, make 9 copies of foundation A and 18 copies of foundation B. You can photocopy the patterns, or use my favorite method of needlepunching the patterns, referring to "Making Needlepunched Foundations" opposite.

2. For a red-centered block, place a 2" red square, right side up, on the *wrong* side of an A foundation. Position a beige triangle, right side down, with the long raw edge aligned with the edge of the red square so that it extends approximately ¼" over the line between spaces 1 and 2. Turn the paper over to the right side and stitch on the line between spaces 1 and 2. Use a small stitch length and extend the stitching slightly beyond the beginning and end of the line. Turn the foundation over, trim the seam to ¼" if necessary, and press the beige triangle open.

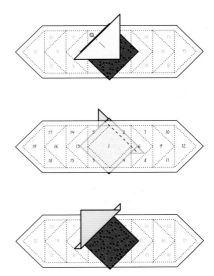

Making Needlepunched Foundations

Needlepunched foundations take a little bit longer to prepare than photocopying all the foundations you need. But, on the back end of your project, you'll easily recoup the time spent because the foundations are so easy to remove. If you've ever avoided foundation piecing because the paper is hard to remove, I encourage you to give this method a try.

1. Make one photocopy of each foundation pattern, and then layer it on top of several sheets of Paper for Foundation Piecing (Martingale & Company). Pin or staple the layers together in a few places, well away from the stitching lines.

2. With no thread in your sewing-machine needle or bobbin, machine stitch along each line of the foundation pattern. This will punch holes into the layers of paper, giving you a clear stitching line as well as perforating your foundation. When it's time to remove the paper, you can tear it away easily because the lines will have been stitched through twice.

3. To avoid any confusion about which fabric goes where, use a pencil or permanent marker to write the piecing order or color on each foundation.

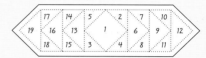

3. Repeat to add a beige triangle on each side of the red center square, following the numerical sequence on the foundation.

4. After all beige triangles have been added around the red square, add a green 3" triangle to spaces 6 and 13 of the foundation. Then add beige triangles to spaces 7, 8, 14, and 15. Remember to trim seams as needed and press the pieces open after each addition.

5. Repeat the process to complete the A foundation, making sure that each piece extends ¼" beyond the marked lines for seam allowances.

6. Make two of foundation B. Using the green 3" triangles and the beige triangles, add them in numerical order. To complete the B foundation, add red triangles cut from the 4¾" squares in spaces 8 and 9.

Foundation B.
Make 2.

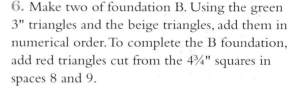

Foundation A.
Make 1.

7. Before sewing the A and B units together, place them one at a time on your cutting mat, paper side up. Using your rotary cutter and ruler, trim away the excess fabric, making sure to leave the ¼" seam allowance beyond the stitching lines all around the foundation.

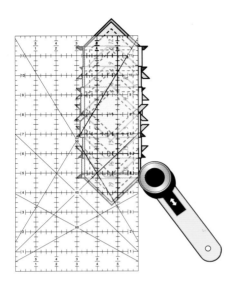

8. Sew a B unit to each long side of the A unit, matching the stitching lines and seam intersections with pins. Remove the paper and press the seam allowances toward the B units.

9. Repeat to make five blocks with red centers and four blocks with green centers.

Make 5.   Make 4.

Assembling the Quilt Top

1. Lay out the blocks in three rows of three blocks each, with the red-centered blocks on the quilt corners and center, alternating with the green-centered blocks.

2. Sew the blocks together into rows and press seams in the opposite direction from row to row.

Sew the rows together. Press the seam allowances to one side.

Quilt layout

Piecing the Borders

1. Cut the 1½" beige border strips into assorted lengths anywhere from 5" to 8" long. Piece the segments together in random order to make one long strip.

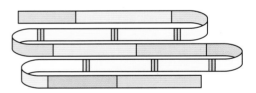

2. From this long strip, cut two strips, 18½" long. Sew these strips to the right and left sides of the quilt top. Cut two more strips, 20½" long, and sew them to the top and bottom of the quilt top.

3. Using the border foundation patterns on page 61, make four foundations with four geese each, four foundations with three geese each, two foundations with two geese each, and two foundations with one geese unit each. Also make four corner foundations.

4. Piece the geese foundations in the same manner as you did for the quilt blocks, randomly selecting 3" red or green triangles and small beige triangles. Piece the four border-corner units using two 2" red squares, two 2" green squares, and the small beige triangles.

5. Assemble the four border strips using the 2½"-wide beige pieces and the pieced flying-geese units as follows. Be sure your geese are all flying in the correct direction as shown.

Top border: 3½" beige piece, three geese, 2½" beige piece, four geese, 4" beige piece, two geese, 3" beige piece.

Bottom border: 2½" beige piece, three geese, 3½" beige piece, two geese, 4" beige piece, four geese, 3" beige piece.

Right border: 2½" beige piece, one geese unit, 3" beige piece, four geese, 5½" beige piece, three geese, 3" beige piece.

Left border: 3½" beige piece, three geese, 4½" beige piece, one geese unit, 3" beige piece, four geese, 3" beige piece.

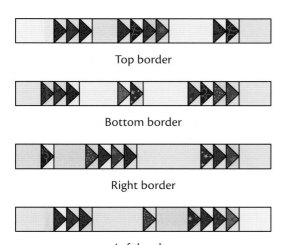

Top border

Bottom border

Right border

Left border

6. Measure the top and bottom pieced borders. If necessary, trim them to fit the width of the quilt top, which should be 20½". Sew these borders to the quilt with the geese pointing toward the right on the top of the quilt and toward the left on the bottom of the quilt.

7. Measure the right and left borders. They should also measure 20½". Sew a pieced green corner unit to one end and a red corner unit to the other end of each border. Before sewing, check that the red and green units will be in opposite corners of the quilt. The geese should be circling the quilt when all borders have been attached. Sew the borders to the sides of the quilt, with the geese pointing downward on the right and upward on the left. Press the quilt top.

Quilt plan

Finishing the Quilt

1. If desired, mark any quilting designs on the quilt top.

2. Place the backing right side down on a table or floor, and lay the batting on top, smoothing out any wrinkles. Then add the pressed quilt top, right side up, on top. Hand or pin baste the layers together.

3. Quilt by hand or machine. The quilt shown was machine quilted in the ditch to outline the X shapes created by the diagonal rows of geese. The inner border was quilted in the ditch along both the inside and outside edges. For the outer border, the geese were quilted in the ditch and the beige pieces were quilted with freeform holly leaves.

4. Using the 2"-wide red strips, make and attach binding, referring to page 9 as needed.

5. If you want to hang your quilt, add a hanging sleeve as described on page 11.

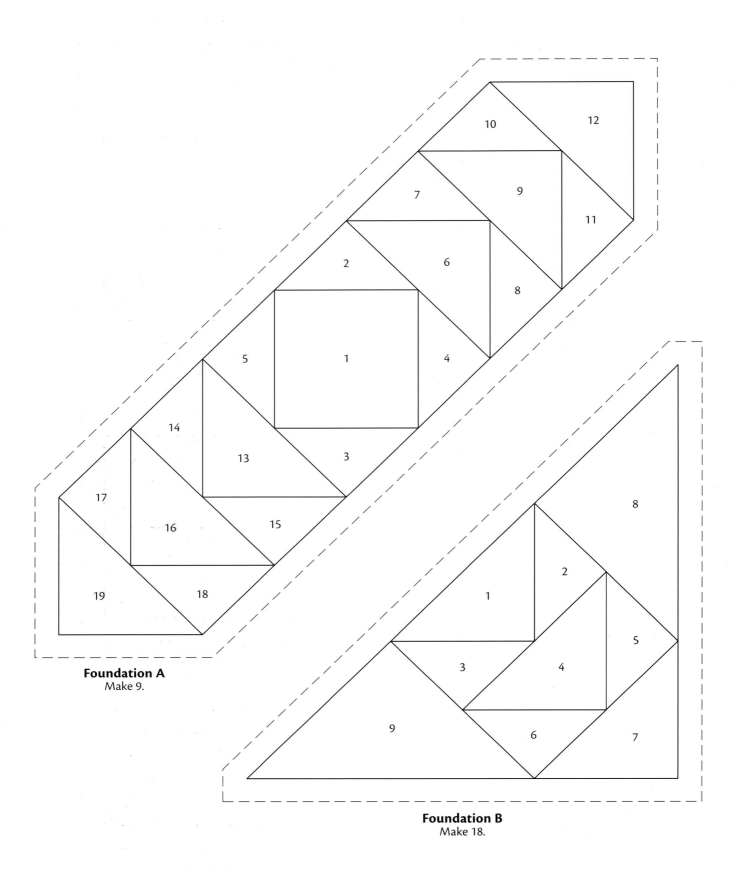

Foundation A
Make 9.

Foundation B
Make 18.

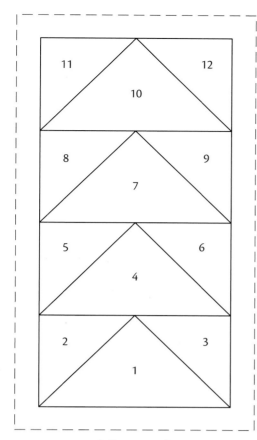

4-Geese unit
Make 4.

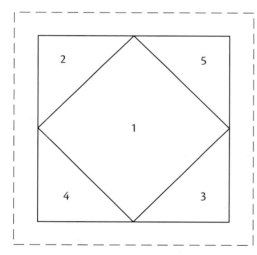

Corner unit
Make 4.

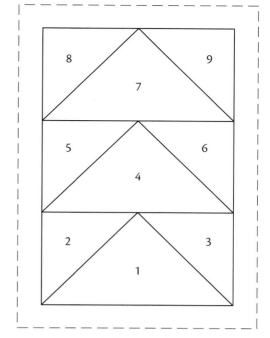

3-Geese unit
Make 4.

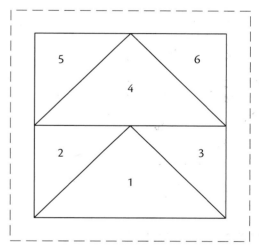

2-Geese unit
Make 2.

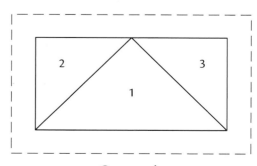

Geese unit
Make 1.

Diamonds

While some quiltmakers think that "triangles" is a bad word, there are others who simply pass right by any pattern that includes diamonds. Why? Probably because diamonds traditionally meant set-in seams and using templates for cutting. You'll be pleasantly surprised to find that none of the three quilt patterns in this chapter require template making or set-in seams. All you need is your rotary cutter and a ruler with 45° and 60° markings on it. Diamond shapes will add interest and versatility to your patchwork repertoire, so don't toss them aside. To paraphrase Marilyn Monroe in *Gentlemen Prefer Blondes*, diamonds can be your best friend!

12-Karat Four Patch

Blue and yellow is a perennial favorite color combination among quilters. When I spied a collection of reproduction indigo prints, I just knew that somehow I had to work yellow into the quilt! The soft yellow sets off the diamond-shaped Four Patch blocks, yet doesn't overwhelm them. Whatever color scheme you choose, I know you'll find that rotary cutting and strip piecing will make this project a quick and easy one to complete.

Quilt Size: 18" x 22½"
Diamond Block Size: 3⅜" x 6"

Materials

- 1 fat quarter of white print for blocks
- 1 fat quarter of yellow print for setting pieces
- 6 assorted fat eighths of indigo blue prints for blocks and borders
- ⅝ yard of backing fabric★
- 20" x 25" piece of batting

   ★*You can use ⅜ yard if you don't mind a seam in the quilt back.*

Cutting

From the white print, cut:

- 6 strips, 2" x 21"

From *each* of the assorted blue prints, cut:

- 1 strip, 2" x 21" (6 total)

From *each* of 2 assorted blue prints, cut:

- 2 border strips, 2½" x 21" (4 total)

From the remainder of the assorted blue prints, cut:

- 5 binding strips, 2" x 21"

From the yellow print, cut:★

- 2 strips, 3½" x 18"
- 2 strips, 4" x 18"
- 2 rectangles, 2¾" x 4¾"

   ★*Be sure to cut your strips from the shortest length (18"), not the longest (21") to ensure you'll have enough fabric from a fat quarter.*

Piecing the Blocks

1. Staggering the ends of the strips by 2", sew a white strip to a blue strip as shown. Press the seam allowances toward the blue strips. Repeat to make six strip sets.

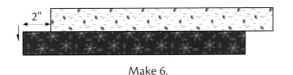

Make 6.

2. Using a rotary cutter and a ruler with 60° markings, align the 60° line with the seam line of a strip set as shown. Trim off the irregular end of the strip set.

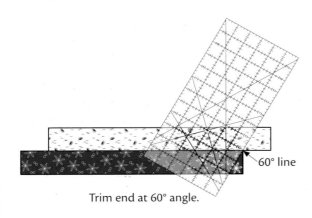

Trim end at 60° angle.

3. Rotate the strip set and measure 2" from the freshly cut end of the strip set; cut a 2"-wide segment. Repeat, cutting at least four 2" segments from each strip set for a total of 24 segments.

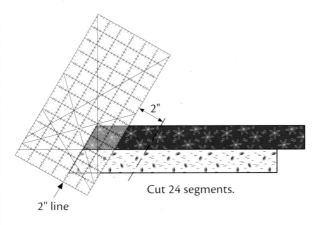

Cut 24 segments.

2" line

4. Select two segments and sew them together to make a diamond four patch; use a pin to match seam intersections. The ends of the patches will be offset as shown. Be sure that you arrange the segments so that the white print makes the sharp point and the blue prints create the wider-angle points. Notice in the quilt shown that some four patches have matching blue fabrics and some don't. Repeat to make 12 blocks.

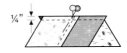

Make 12.

Assembling the Quilt Top

1. Lay a 3½"-wide yellow strip on your cutting mat. Position the 60° line of the ruler along the lower cut edge of the strip. Cut along the edge of the ruler to create the angled end of the strip. Then rotate the strip and measure 3½" from the freshly cut edge; cut again to make a diamond. Repeat to cut six diamonds.

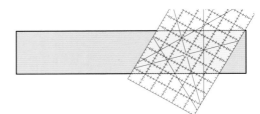

Trim end at 60° angle.

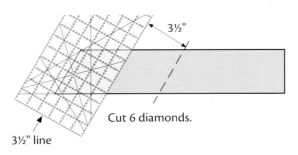

3½"

Cut 6 diamonds.

3½" line

Machine pieced and hand quilted by author.

2. To cut the partial diamonds for setting pieces, cut 4" diamonds from the 4" yellow strips in the same manner, using the 60° and 4" lines on your ruler. Cut five of these diamonds. Cut three of them in half horizontally to make half-diamonds for the top and bottom rows of the quilt. Cut two of them in half vertically to make half-diamonds for the sides of the quilt. Cut the two yellow rectangles in half diagonally as shown to make the four corner triangles. *Note:* The setting triangles are slightly oversize; they will be trimmed when you square up your quilt top before adding the borders.

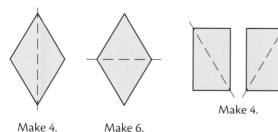

Make 4. Make 6. Make 4.

Go with the Grain

When placing the top and bottom setting triangles, look at the fabric pieces to find the straight grain. Place the triangles so that the straight grain will be along the outer edge of the quilt top.

3. Arrange the four-patch diamonds and yellow diamonds in rows. Fill in the gaps with the side, top, bottom, and corner setting triangles.

4. Sew the pieces together into diagonal rows, off-setting the pieces as before. Press the seams toward the yellow diamonds and setting triangles. Sew the rows together, matching the seam intersections with pins. Press the seam allowances in one direction. Add the corner triangles last, pressing the seam allowances toward the yellow triangles.

Quilt layout

5. Square up the quilt top, leaving ¼" beyond all the points of the blocks.

6. Measure the width of the quilt top; it should be approximately 14½". Trim two of the 2½"-wide blue strips to this length and sew them to the top and bottom of the quilt. Press the seam allowances toward the borders. *Note:* In the quilt shown, two different fabrics were used for the top and bottom borders.

7. For the side borders, measure the length of the quilt top; it should be approximately 22½". You'll need to piece these borders. I used a diagonal seam to diminish the appearance of the seams and to echo the diagonal lines of the patchwork in the quilt. After piecing two border strips, trim each to the length of your quilt top and join them to the sides of the quilt. Press the seam allowances toward the borders.

Quilt plan

Finishing the Quilt

1. If desired, mark any quilting designs on the quilt top.

2. Piece the quilt backing if necessary and press the seam allowance to one side. Place the backing right side down on a table or floor, and lay the batting on top, smoothing out any wrinkles. Then add the pressed quilt top, right side up, on top. Hand or pin baste the layers together.

3. Quilt by hand or machine. The quilt shown was hand quilted. Using masking tape as a guide, I quilted the pieced diamonds ¼" inside the perimeter of each four patch, and then bisected the squares with quilting for an argyle affect. I quilted the yellow diamonds with three concentric diamonds.

4. Using the 2"-wide blue strips, make and attach binding, referring to page 9 as needed.

5. If you want to hang your quilt, add a hanging sleeve as described on page 11.

Antique Diamonds

This scrappy quilt is made from a wide assortment of Civil War—era reproduction fabrics. Some of these fabrics are bold with wild prints; others are much more subtle. You can make this easy diamond quilt using any color palette with fabrics representing any era—even thoroughly modern bright colors that kids would love. Sort through your scrap bag or basket for strips that are at least 2" wide. I used at least 30 fabrics for this little gem that doesn't even measure 30" tall. The more, the merrier!

Quilt Size: 24" x 25"

Materials

- 30 assorted 2"-wide strips, at least 21" long, for diamonds
- ⅓ yard of blue print for outer border
- 2 red or pink print strips, 2" x 21", for inner border
- 1 fat quarter of dark blue print for binding
- ⅞ yard of backing fabric
- 26" x 27" piece of batting

★ *Strips can be fat-quarter length (21") or longer.*

Machine pieced and hand quilted by author.

Cutting

From the assorted fabric strips, trim each strip:

- 2" wide x varying lengths (from 21" to 42")

From the blue print, cut:

- 2 border strips, 3" x 21"
- 2 border strips, 3¼" x 24"

From the dark blue print, cut:

- 6 strips, 2" x 21"

Piecing the Chevron Strips

1. Randomly select three 2" strips. Staggering the ends by 2" each, sew the strips together along their long edges. Press all seam allowances in one direction. Repeat to make five strip sets staggered to the right and five sets staggered to the left.

Make 5 strip sets.

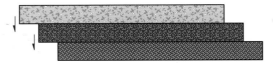

Make 5 strip sets.

2. Using a rotary cutter and a ruler with 45° markings, align the 45° line with the seam line of a strip set as shown. Trim off the irregular end of the strip set.

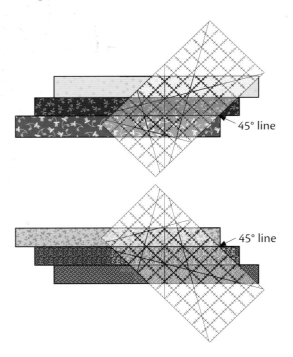

3. Rotate the strip set 180°. Measure 2" from the freshly cut end of the strip set and cut a 2"-wide segment. Repeat, cutting 2" segments from all strip sets for a total of 36 segments.

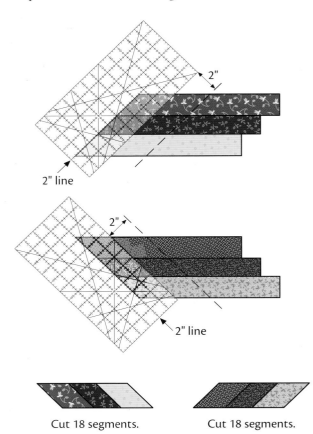

Cut 18 segments.   Cut 18 segments.

4. Sew three segments together end to end to make one strip for the chevron. Repeat, making a total of six strip sets slanting in each direction. Press all seams in one direction.

Make 6.

Make 6.

5. Lay out the strips side by side, placing them so that the diamonds slant in opposite directions from one strip to the next and rotating them so seam allowances will butt together. When you are pleased with the color arrangement, pin to match seam intersections, and then stitch the strips together.

Trim the ends of the quilt center to square it up. Make sure you leave ¼" of fabric past the last seam intersection for the seam allowance.

Trim ends to square up.

6. Measure the width of the quilt top; it should be 18½". Trim the two pink or red strips to this length. Sew the strips to the top and bottom of the quilt. Press the seam allowances toward the border strips.

7. Measure the length of the quilt top; it should be 18½". Trim the two narrower of the blue border strips to this length. Sew the strips to the sides of the quilt top and press the seam allowance toward the blue borders.

8. In the same manner, measure the width of the quilt top; it should be 23½". Trim the remaining blue borders to this length, and attach them to the top and bottom of the quilt. Press.

Quilt layout

Finishing the Quilt

1. If desired, mark any quilting designs on the quilt top.

2. Place the backing right side down on a table or floor, and lay the batting on top, smoothing out any wrinkles. Then add the pressed quilt top, right side up, on top. Hand or pin baste the layers together.

3. Quilt by hand or machine. The quilt shown was hand quilted ¼" inside each diamond. The pink borders are quilted in a series of three parallel straight lines at each seam line in the chevron pattern. The outer border is quilted with a large cross-hatching pattern.

4. Using the 2"-wide dark blue strips, make and attach binding, referring to page 9 as needed.

5. If you want to hang your quilt, add a hanging sleeve as described on page 11.

Pennsylvania Star

During my very first quilt class, we made a block called Summer Star. I loved the way the center star is completely set inside the larger star. At that time, we made the block using templates to cut the diamond shapes, as well as the triangles. Now, I've redrafted the block and made it suitable for foundation piecing. There are no set-in seams, and each wedge of the block has just five pieces. I used traditional Pennsylvania Dutch colors: chrome yellow, bright red, and the closest thing I could find to a traditional fabric called "Pennsylvania blue," the same colors used in the pillows on page 74 made from an antique quilt. To complete my ode to my home state, I used heart and tulip quilting motifs, popular in quilts, Frakturs, hex signs, and other regional artwork.

Quilt Size: 17½" x 17½"
Block Size: 14" x 14"

Materials

❖ 1 fat quarter of bright yellow print for block and border

❖ 1 fat quarter of bright red print for block and binding

❖ 1 fat quarter of medium to light blue for block background

❖ ⅝ yard of backing fabric★

❖ 20" x 20" piece of batting

★*You can use ⅜ yard if you don't mind a seam in your quilt back.*

Machine pieced and machine quilted by author.

Cutting

From the yellow print, cut:
❖ 4 border strips, 2" x 21"
❖ 2 strips, 2¼" x 21"

From the red print, cut:
❖ 4 binding strips, 2" x 21"
❖ 4 strips, 2¼" x 21"

From the blue print, cut:
❖ 4 squares, 5" x 5"; cut in half diagonally to yield 8 triangles
❖ 4 squares, 6" x 6"; cut in half diagonally to yield 8 triangles

Piecing the Block

Make four copies each of the A and B foundations on page 77 by photocopying or referring to "Making Needlepunched Foundations" on page 57. Each quadrant of the block uses one A and one B foundation. However, because you'll be cutting the red and yellow strips on an angle, you'll make best use of your fabric if you piece all the A units first, and then make all the B units using the remaining fabric strips.

1. Place a 2¼"-wide yellow strip on the wrong side of the foundation paper with the right side of the fabric facing up, making sure that it extends beyond the seam line on all sides. Place a 2¼"-wide red strip with the right side facing the yellow strip as shown. Turn the paper over and stitch on the marked line between spaces 1 and 2. Open up the red fabric, press in place, and trim the excess yellow and red fabric. Make sure to leave ¼" of red fabric extending beyond the line between spaces 2 and 5 for the seam allowance.

3. Using a 6" blue triangle, position and sew it to the line between spaces 3 and 4. Before sewing, pin along the marked line, flip open the blue triangle, and make sure that it will cover the entire patch as well as the exterior seam allowances.

4. Finish the foundation unit by adding a 4" blue triangle in space 5 in the same manner.

5. Place the foundation, paper side up, on your cutting mat. Using a rotary cutter and ruler, trim the excess fabric from the block, being sure to leave a ¼" seam allowance on all sides of the pieced triangle. Repeat to make four A and four B foundations.

6. Lay out the foundations, pairing an A and a B foundation for each quadrant of the block. Stitch the A and B pieces together in pairs to make a quadrant. Press the seam allowances open. Then sew the squares together in pairs and, finally, sew the pairs together. Remove the paper foundations and press the block. The quilt block should measure 14½" square.

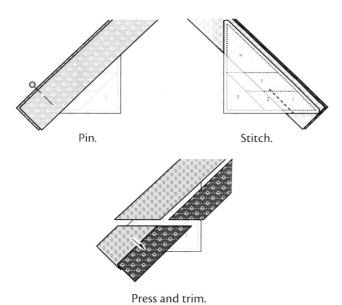

Pin.   Stitch.

Press and trim.

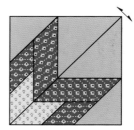

Sew A to B; press seams open.
Make 4.

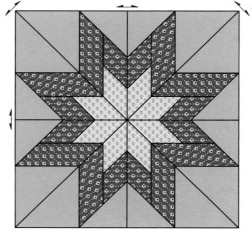

Press all seams open.

2. Place the red strip wrong side up and with the right side facing pieces 1 and 2; position it so that the edge is ¼" beyond the line that separates space 3 from spaces 1 and 2. Turn the foundation over and stitch on the line. Open up the red fabric, press, and trim excess fabric as before.

Adding the Mitered Border

The quilt block should measure 14½" x 14½". Measure to be sure.

1. Using your rotary cutter and a ruler marked with a 45° line, trim one end of each yellow border strip at a 45° angle.

2. For a perfect-fit border, measure 14½" from the inside angle (the edge that will be adjacent to your quilt top) and make a pencil mark at the edge of the border. Align your ruler to cut the opposite end of the strip at a 45° angle, this time angling the ruler in the opposite direction as shown. Repeat for all four border strips.

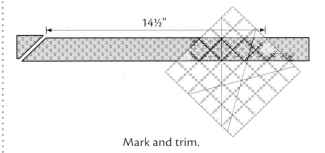

Mark and trim.

3. Pin a border to one side of the quilt, aligning the 14½" edge with the edge of the quilt top and matching the ends of the border strip with the ends of the quilt top. Pin at the centers and add additional pins as necessary. Stitch the border to the quilt top, starting and stopping ¼" from each end, and press the seam allowance toward the border. Repeat for all four borders.

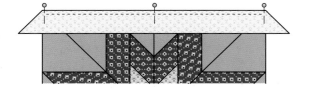

4. To finish the corners, align the angled ends of two adjacent border strips, right sides facing, and pin. Stitch this short seam, starting ¼" from the inside edge and sewing to the ends of the strips. Trim the dog-ears at the outer corner of the border strips, press the seam open, and then repeat for the remaining corners.

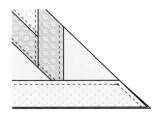

Finishing the Quilt

1. If desired, mark any quilting designs on the quilt top.

2. If necessary, piece the quilt backing and press the seam to one side. Place the backing right side down on a table or floor, and lay the batting on top, smoothing out any wrinkles. Then add the pressed quilt top, right side up, on top. Hand or pin baste the layers together.

3. Quilt by hand or machine. The quilt shown was machine quilted in the ditch around the yellow star. The star shape was echo quilted in the interior of the yellow star as well as in the red star by using the edge of the walking foot on the machine as a guide. A simple tulip shape was quilted in the four corners and a heart was quilted in the blue triangle shapes. An easy way to make motifs like this is to cut them out of freezer paper, iron them in place on the quilt, stitch around the paper motif, and then peel away the paper. No marks to remove.

4. Using the 2"-wide red strips, make and attach binding, referring to page 9 as needed.

5. If you want to hang your quilt, add a hanging sleeve as described on page 11.

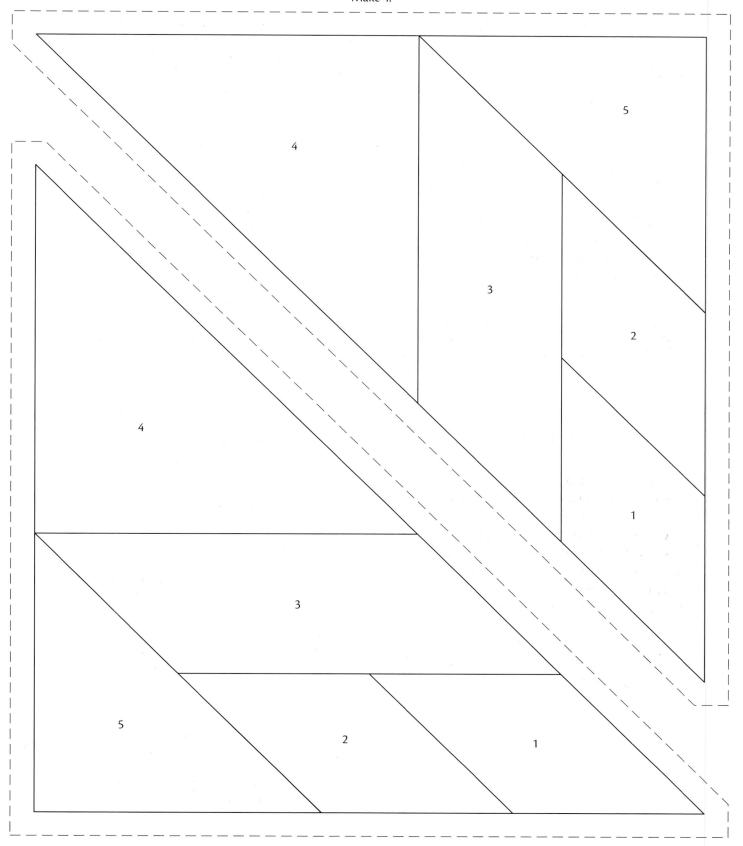

Curves and Circles with Easy Appliqué

When I first started quilting, appliqué was something I never planned to do. Up to that point, my only experience with hand sewing had to do with mending and hemming. Can you blame me for not wanting to learn appliqué?

Today I thoroughly enjoy appliqué. It lets you add shapes and designs to quilts that would be impossible to accomplish with piecing. And there are so many ways to appliqué, whether you prefer to do it by hand or by machine. In this book, I've included just three examples of appliqué. Two are done by hand, but they could just as easily be fused and stitched by machine if that's your preference. The other is fused and securely held in place with a decorative machine blanket stitch. I think you'll find any of the three projects totally manageable and easy to accomplish even for appliqué novices.

Japanese Circles

I love to browse through Japanese quilting magazines. I often wish that I could read the articles and the directions for the fabulous quilts and other projects that these publications hold. But even though I can't read a word, *Quilt Japan* and *Patchwork Tsushin* offer a world of inspiration. This little quilt is just one example. In one issue I noticed a picture of a variety of purses, totes, and duffels, all intricately stitched. The flap of one purse really caught my eye: it had a variety of fabric circles appliquéd to alternating black and brown squares, much like a checkerboard. It stuck in my mind, and eventually this little quilt was born.

Quilt Size: 17½" x 20½"
Block Size: 3" x 3"

Materials

- ½ yard of brown subtle print for blocks and borders
- 1 fat quarter of brown stripe for blocks
- Scraps of 20 colored fabrics, about 6" x 6" each, for appliqués and pieced border
- ⅝ yard of backing fabric
- 20" x 23" piece of batting
- 3" square of template plastic
- Freezer paper
- Fine-point permanent marker
- White embroidery thread (optional)

Cutting

From the brown print, cut:
- 10 squares, 3½" x 3½"
- 2 border strips, 1" x 42"
- 2 border strips, 1½" x 42"
- 31 squares, 1½" x 1½"

From the brown stripe, cut:
- 10 squares, 3½" x 3½"

From the colored scraps, cut:
- 31 squares, 1½" x 1½"

Appliquéing the Blocks

1. Make a plastic template using the circle pattern on page 83. Trace the pattern onto the dull side of freezer paper 20 times using the fine-point marker. Cut out the freezer-paper templates exactly on the drawn line.

2. Press the freezer-paper circles onto the wrong side of the colored fabric scraps. Cut out each circle, leaving a scant ¼" (or less) seam allowance. Hand baste a ring of gathering stitches around the paper, sewing in the seam allowance area. Pull the thread to gather the seam allowance over the edge of the paper. Hand baste the seam allowance in place, stitching through both paper and fabric. Ease in the excess fabric as you go. The narrower the seam allowance, the easier it will be to ease in the fabric. Press.

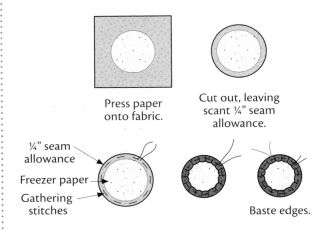

Press paper onto fabric.

Cut out, leaving scant ¼" seam allowance.

¼" seam allowance

Freezer paper

Gathering stitches

Baste edges.

3. Fold a brown fabric square in half vertically and horizontally and finger-press to mark the center. Fold a circle in half in the same manner and crease. Matching the vertical and horizontal creases, center the circle on the brown square and pin in place.

Match centers and pin in place.

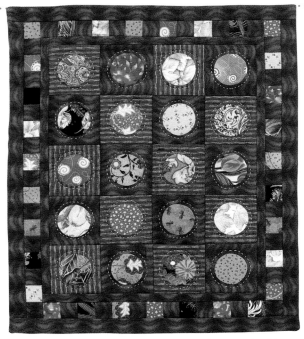

Designed, pieced, and hand and machine quilted by author; hand appliquéd by Karen Clifton, Monroe, Washington.

4. Appliqué the circle in place using a small invisible stitch and thread to match the appliqué fabric. When you have about 1" to go, remove the basting stitches, pull out the freezer paper with tweezers (or fingers), fold the seam allowance back under the appliqué, and finish stitching in place.

5. Repeat steps 2–4 to make 20 blocks, 10 using the brown print background squares and 10 using the brown stripe squares.

Assembling the Quilt Top

1. Lay out the appliquéd squares in five rows of four blocks each, alternating the background fabrics. When you are satisfied with the color arrangement, sew the blocks together into rows. Press the seam allowances in opposite directions from one row to the next. Then sew the rows together and press the seam allowances in one direction.

2. Measure the length of the quilt top through the middle; it should measure 15½". Cut a 1" brown print strip into two strips of this length. Sew the strips to the sides of the quilt top and press the seam allowances toward the brown borders. Measure the width of the quilt; it should measure 13½". Cut the remaining 1" brown print strip into two strips of that length. Sew them to the top and bottom of the quilt and press.

3. To make the top and bottom pieced borders, lay out the 1½" brown and colored squares, alternating them. The top border starts and ends with colored squares. The bottom border starts and ends with brown squares. Each border has a total of 13 squares. Sew the squares together; press the seams in one direction. Sew these borders to the quilt and press the seam allowances toward the brown inner border.

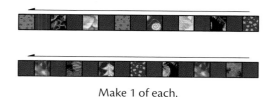

Make 1 of each.

4. Make two side borders with 18 squares each, alternating brown and colored 1½" squares. Press the seam allowances in one direction. Add these borders to the sides of the quilt, positioning them so that the brown squares are next to a colored square in the top and bottom borders. Press the seam allowances toward the brown inner border.

Make 2.

5. Measure the length of the quilt top; it should be 18½". Cut the 1½" brown print border strip into two strips of this length. Join them to the sides of the quilt and press the seam allowances toward the brown border. Measure the width of the quilt in the same manner; it should be 17½". Cut two strips to fit from the remaining brown print strip. Sew them to the top and bottom of the quilt, and press.

Finishing the Quilt

1. If desired, mark any quilting designs on the quilt top.

2. Trim the backing fabric to the same size as the quilt top. Place the batting on the table or floor, smoothing out any wrinkles. Layer the pressed quilt top on the batting, right side up. Finally, add the quilt backing, right side down, on top. Smooth and pin the layers together around the perimeter.

Using a walking foot on your machine, stitch around the perimeter of the quilt with a ¼" seam allowance. Leave an opening on one side for turning. Trim the excess batting from the corners and turn the quilt right side out. Smooth out any wrinkles, press the edges flat, and hand stitch the opening closed.

3. Baste the layers and quilt by hand or machine. The quilt shown was machine quilted in the ditch between the blocks and along the border seam lines to hold everything in place. Then, using one strand of white embroidery floss, stitching was added around the appliquéd circles using a longer-than-normal quilting stitch to simulate the look of sashiko (traditional Japanese quilting).

4. If you want to hang your quilt, add a hanging sleeve as described on page 11.

2" circle
Pattern does not include seam allowance. Add ⅛" to ¼" seam allowance for needle-turn appliqué.

Maple Sugar Hearts

Inspiration can come from many places. One night when I was having trouble sleeping, I decided to browse through some decorating books. Near the back of one old book I noticed a black-and-white photograph of an antique wooden mold used to make maple sugar candy hearts. The photo was small and very dark, but the pattern of the hearts, alternating in direction to fit as many as possible on the carved plank of wood, made the old tool much more interesting than if the hearts all marched right-side-up across the mold. A selection of pink and red florals, checks, and stripes brings the hearts to life on a subtle brown background.

Quilt Size: 19½" x 23½"

Materials

- 1 fat quarter of medium brown print for background
- 1 fat quarter of light stripe for inner border
- 1 fat quarter of dark brown print for outer border
- 1 fat quarter of dark brown print for binding
- Scraps (3½" x 4½") of 20 assorted pink and red florals, checks, and stripes for hearts
- ⅔ yard of backing fabric
- 23" x 27" piece of batting
- 3½" x 4" piece of template plastic
- Fine-point permanent marker

Cutting

From the light stripe, cut:
- 4 strips, 1¼" x 21"
- 5 binding strips, 2" x 21"

From the dark brown print, cut:
- 4 border strips, 3" x 21"

Appliquéing the Quilt Top

1. Using the pattern on page 88, trace the heart onto template plastic and cut out exactly on the line. Trace around the template on the right side of each of the pink or red scraps using the fine-point permanent marker. Cut out the hearts, cutting ⅛" to ¼" outside the drawn line.

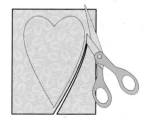

Cut out, leaving
⅛" seam allowance.

2. Mark placement lines on the background fabric for the hearts. To avoid marking with a pencil, simply fold the fabric in half lengthwise and press a crease. This will be the line for the center row of hearts. Mark additional vertical placement lines by measuring 2½" from the center crease, fold the fabric along these lines, and press. Continue in this fashion, creasing five vertical placement lines.

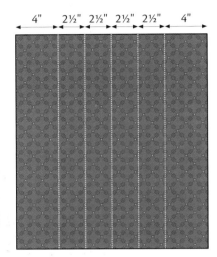

Fold and press
to mark placement lines.

3. Place the first heart along the left placement line, positioning it about 2" from the top of the fabric. Pin or baste in place. Appliqué in place using the needle-turn method and a thread color that matches the appliqué fabric. Beginning on a straight side of the heart, use your needle to turn under ½" or so of the edge of the heart. Hold the turned-under edge with the thumb of your non-sewing hand and stitch the folded edge in place with a small stitch.

Continue turning under just a bit at a time, trimming the seam allowance if necessary as you go. The narrower the seam allowance, the easier it will be to make a smooth curve at the top of the heart and a narrow point at the bottom. When you reach the point where you started stitching, knot the thread on the wrong side of the fabric behind the appliqué.

Tips for Needle-Turn Appliqué

❖ Start with a ⅛" to ¼" seam allowance when you cut out the appliqués, but trim them narrower as you go. That way, you'll have a narrow seam allowance that is easier to turn under smoothly, and you'll have a freshly cut edge when you're ready to appliqué—no frayed edges.

❖ Start stitching along the straight edge of the heart, not on the curve or right by the bottom point.

❖ When you reach the inner point at the top of the heart, use a small, sharp pair of scissors to snip perpendicularly to the marked line. Then splay the two sides of the seam allowance to fall beneath the two curves of the heart.

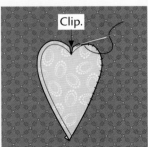

Clip.

❖ For the bottom point, stitch the first side completely to the point. Take an extra stitch at the point, and then sweep the seam allowance along the next side under the point. Pull your stitching taut to make a sharp point, but not so tightly that it puckers.

4. Place the second heart below the first one so that the bottom point of the first heart is 1" from the inner point at the top of the second heart. Appliqué in place as for the first heart. Continue positioning and appliquéing the row in this manner.

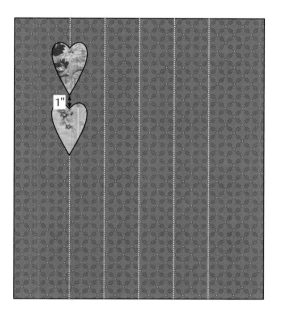

5. For the second row, the hearts will be placed facing in the opposite direction. The vertical center of the hearts should be aligned with the crease, and the top and bottom of each heart should be aligned with the hearts in the first row.

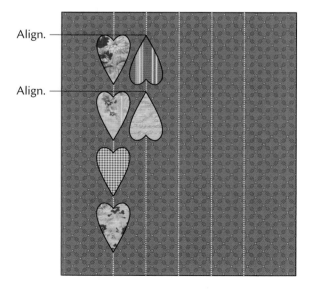

Designed, appliquéd, and hand quilted by author.

6. When all hearts have been appliquéd, press the quilt top from the wrong side. Square up the quilt, measuring 1" from the edges of the hearts to the edge of the fabric. I trimmed to 14½" x 18½".

7. Fold the 1¼" light strips in half lengthwise, *wrong* sides together. Machine baste a strip to each long side of the quilt using a scant ¼" seam allowance. Then baste the remaining two strips to the short sides of the quilt. Trim the excess fabric.

Baste and trim.

8. Measure the length of the quilt top. Trim two of the dark brown border strips to this length. Sew them to the sides of the quilt and press the seam allowances toward the brown borders. The striped strips should lie flat, pressed toward the hearts. In the same manner, measure the width of the quilt and trim the remaining two dark brown strips to this measurement. Sew them to the top and bottom of the quilt. Press.

Faux Miters

When I basted the light strips to the quilt top and bottom, I folded the corners back at a 45° angle to create the look of a mitered corner. This worked well with the stripe print that I had chosen.

Finishing the Quilt

1. If desired, mark any quilting designs on the quilt top.

2. Place the backing right side down on a table or floor, and lay the batting on top, smoothing out any wrinkles. Then add the pressed quilt top, right side up, on top. Hand or pin baste the layers together.

3. Quilt by hand or machine. The quilt shown was hand quilted, stitching about $1/16$" outside each heart. The background was quilted in diagonal lines. The border was quilted with a swag to complement the curves in the hearts. I used a coffee mug, a small dish, and a chalk pencil to mark the curved lines.

4. Using the 2"-wide light stripe strips, make and attach binding, referring to page 9 as needed.

5. If you want to hang your quilt, add a hanging sleeve as described on page 11.

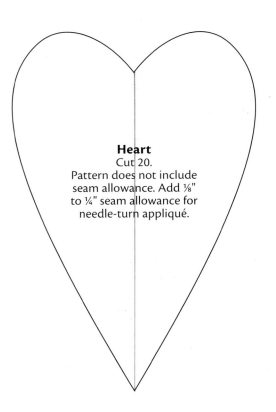

Heart
Cut 20.
Pattern does not include
seam allowance. Add 1/8"
to 1/4" seam allowance for
needle-turn appliqué.

Sweet Pea

What little girl wouldn't love a sweet little quilt for her dolls? Fusible appliqué that's machine blanket stitched is not only easy to do but quite durable, too, making it a good choice for a doll quilt that will be played with frequently.

Quilt Size: 18" x 25"
Block Size: 6½" x 6½"

Materials

- ❖ 1 fat quarter *each* of a small-scale and a medium-scale yellow print for blocks and sashing
- ❖ 1 fat quarter of light blue print for quarter circles and sashing squares
- ❖ 1 fat eighth *each* or scraps of pink print and green print for floral appliqués
- ❖ 1 fat quarter of light blue tone-on-tone print for border
- ❖ 1 fat quarter of pink floral print for binding
- ❖ ⅝ yard of backing fabric
- ❖ 20" x 27" piece of batting
- ❖ ½ yard of lightweight fusible web
- ❖ Blue, pink, and green thread to match appliqué fabrics

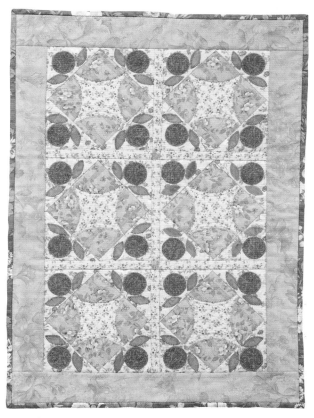

Machine pieced, machine appliquéd, and machine quilted by author.

Preparing Appliqué Shapes

Using the patterns on page 93, trace 6 large circles, 24 small circles, and 48 leaves onto the paper side of fusible web. Group like shapes together on the fusible web so that you can fuse them as a single unit to the wrong side of the fabrics. Fuse the large circles onto the blue print fabric, the small circles onto the pink print, and the leaves onto the green print.

Cutting

From the light blue print, cut:
- ❖ 6 large circles, prepared with fusible web
- ❖ 2 squares, 1" x 1"

From the small-scale yellow print, cut:
- ❖ 6 squares, 5" x 5"
- ❖ 7 strips, 1" x 7"

From the medium-scale yellow print, cut:

- 12 squares, 4¼" x 4¼"; cut in half diagonally to yield 24 triangles

From the pink print, cut:

- 24 small circles, prepared with fusible web

From the green print, cut:

- 48 leaves, prepared with fusible web

From the light blue tone-on-tone print, cut:

- 4 border strips, 2½" x 21"

From the pink floral print, cut:

- 5 binding strips, 2" x 21"

Making the Blocks

1. After cutting out the large blue circles on the drawn lines, fold each circle in half and crease. Cut the circles in half on the creases. Then fold the semicircles in half again, crease, and cut into quarter circles.

Cut circles
into quarters.

Tips for Easy Blanket Stitching

❖ Lessen the thread tension on your machine so that the bobbin thread won't show on top. You can use the same thread you use for piecing in the bobbin and just change the color on top where it will show.

❖ All the shapes in the piece are curved, so you'll need to lift the presser foot and turn the fabric every few stitches so that the stitch that bites into the appliqué shape will be perpendicular to the edge of the appliqué, not slanted.

❖ When stitching points, take one stitch on each side of the point, and one directly at the point, turning the fabric each time so that the stitching looks similar to that shown at right.

Stitch perpendicularly
at points.

❖ I find it's not necessary to use a stabilizer since the fusible web has stiffened the fabric enough to support the stitches. However, if you have trouble with your machine as it stitches from a single layer of fabric to the fused appliqué layer, a sheet of tissue paper or other tear-away stabilizer can be used. Using a slim machine-embroidery or machine-quilting needle will also help.

❖ Don't cut the threads between the quarter circles within one block. You'll save time and thread if you simply lift the presser foot and needle, slide the block into position for stitching the next quarter circle, and continuing with your stitching.

2. Remove the paper backing and fuse a quarter circle onto each corner of a 5" yellow square, aligning cut edges in the corners of the block. Machine blanket stitch the curved edges in place using blue thread. Repeat for all six blocks.

Fuse and blanket
stitch into place.

3. Sew a yellow triangle to opposite sides of an appliquéd block. Press the seam allowances toward the triangles. Sew remaining triangles to each of the two remaining sides of the block and press in the same manner. Repeat to make six blocks. Trim and square up the blocks to 7" x 7".

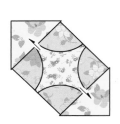 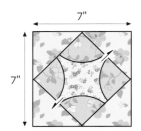

Make 6.

4. Remove the paper backing from the pink circles and leaves. Place one pink circle and two leaves in each corner triangle, taking care to position the pieces so that they will not extend into the outer ¼" seam allowance of the block. When satisfied with the placement, fuse in place. Machine blanket stitch around each shape with coordinating thread. Repeat for all six blocks.

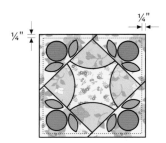

Fuse circles and leaves
¼" away from block edges.

Assembling the Quilt Top

1. Lay out the quilt blocks in three rows of two blocks each. Place 1" x 7" yellow sashing strips between the blocks, and 1" blue squares between the horizontal sashing strips.

2. Sew the block and sashing pieces into rows, and then sew the rows together, pressing all seam allowances toward the sashing strips.

3. Measure the length of the quilt top; it should be 21". Trim two of the blue border strips to this length and sew them to the sides of the quilt top. Press seam allowances toward the borders. Measure the width of the quilt top; it should be 18". Trim the remaining two border strips to this length and sew them to the top and bottom of the quilt in the same manner.

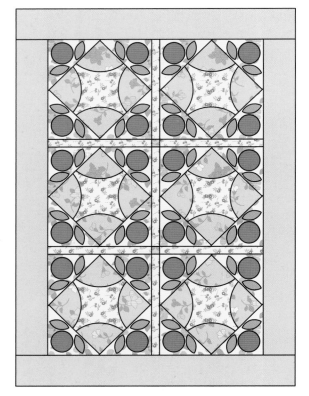

Quilt plan

Finishing

1. If desired, mark any quilting designs on the quilt top.

2. Place the backing right side down on a table or floor, and lay the batting on top, smoothing out any wrinkles. Then add the pressed quilt top, right side up, on top. Hand or pin baste the layers together.

3. Quilt by hand or machine. The quilt shown was machine quilted in the ditch of the seams and about ⅛" or less from the appliquéd pieces—the quarter circles, flower circles, and leaves.

4. Using the 2"-wide pink floral strips, make and attach binding, referring to page 9 as needed.

5. If you want to hang your quilt, add a hanging sleeve as described on page 11.

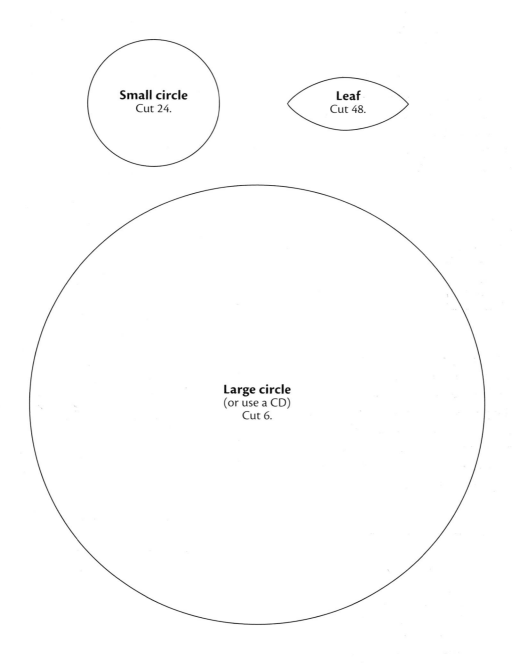

Small circle
Cut 24.

Leaf
Cut 48.

Large circle
(or use a CD)
Cut 6.

Acknowledgments

Many of my quilting friends have helped me in one way or another with this book. Some contributed beautiful stitching, some provided inspiration, others offered encouragement, and some may not even know that they helped—but the many lessons learned from them over the years have helped my quiltmaking to grow and improve, and to each of you, I thank you.

Special thanks to the following:

- Karen Clifton, for appliquéing the "Japanese Circles" quilt.

- Shannon Camardo, for stitching all those dozens of foundation-pieced triangles and improvising the border design for the "Christmas Goose" quilt.

- Nancy Johnson-Srebro and Karen Bolesta, longtime friends who pieced the "One Patch Garden" quilt as a going-away gift. I miss our retreats!

- Ellen Pahl, another longtime friend, for daily email chats and inspiration, for editing this book, and for bringing an artful eye to styling the photographs.

- Beth Kovich, for lending me her adorable vintage bow tie quilt for so long.

- Robin Strobel, for her beautiful illustrations that perfectly capture the spirit of my little quilts.

- Patricia Field, for her creative book design.

About the Author

Karen Costello Soltys has been quilting since 1979 when she took her first quilting class from Susan Aylsworth Murwin, coauthor of *Quick and Easy Patchwork on the Sewing Machine* (Dover, 1979). Since then, Karen has made countless quilts for family, friends, and charitable causes, mostly using machine techniques, but also including hand appliqué and hand quilting. While she has contributed quilts to other authors' books and edited many quilting books over the past 15 years, this is the first book she has authored.

Karen also enjoys rug hooking, knitting, and basketmaking. Originally from southeastern Pennsylvania, she currently lives in western Washington.

New and Bestselling Titles from

America's Best-Loved Craft & Hobby Books®
America's Best-Loved Knitting Books®

America's Best-Loved Quilt Books®

APPLIQUÉ
Adoration Quilts
Appliqué at Play
Appliqué Takes Wing
Favorite Quilts from Anka's Treasures
Garden Party
Mimi Dietrich's Baltimore Basics
Stitch and Split Appliqué
Sunbonnet Sue and Scottie Too—*New!*
Tea in the Garden

FOCUS ON WOOL
Hooked on Wool
Needle Felting—*New!*
Simply Primitive

GENERAL QUILTMAKING
All Buttoned Up
Bound for Glory—*New!*
Calendar Kids
Colorful Quilts—*New!*
Creating Your Perfect Quilting Space
Creative Quilt Collection Volume Two
Dazzling Quilts
A Dozen Roses—*New!*
Follow-the-Line Quilting Designs
Follow-the-Line Quilting Designs
    Volume Two
A Fresh Look at Seasonal Quilts
Modern Primitive Quilts—*New!*
Positively Postcards—*New!*
Posterize It!—*New!*
Prairie Children and Their Quilts
Quilt Revival
Quilter's Block-a-Day Calendar—*New!*
Quilting in the Country—*New!*
Sensational Sashiko
Simple Traditions
Twice Quilted—*New!*

LEARNING TO QUILT
The Blessed Home Quilt
Color for the Terrified Quilter—*New!*
Happy Endings, Revised Edition
Let's Quilt!
The Magic of Quiltmaking
The Quilter's Quick Reference Guide
Your First Quilt Book (or it should be!)

PAPER PIECING
300 Paper-Pieced Quilt Blocks
Easy Machine Paper Piecing
Show Me How to Paper Piece
**Showstopping Quilts to
    Foundation Piece—*New!***
Spellbinding Quilts

PIECING
40 Fabulous Quick-Cut Quilts
Better by the Dozen
Big 'n Easy
Clever Quarters, Too
Lickety-Split Quilts
New Cuts for New Quilts
Over Easy
Sew One and You're Done
Snowball Quilts
Square Deal—*New!*
Stack a New Deck
Sudoku Quilts
Two-Block Theme Quilts
Twosey-Foursey Quilts
Wheel of Mystery Quilts

QUILTS FOR BABIES & CHILDREN
Even More Quilts for Baby
**The Little Box of Baby Quilts
    —*New!***
More Quilts for Baby
Quilts for Baby
Sweet and Simple Baby Quilts

SCRAP QUILTS
More Nickel Quilts
Nickel Quilts
Save the Scraps
Scraps of Time
Simple Strategies for Scrap Quilts
Successful Scrap Quilts from Simple
    Rectangles
A Treasury of Scrap Quilts

CRAFTS
Bag Boutique
Creative Embellishments—*New!*
Greeting Cards Using Digital Photos
It's a Wrap
**The Little Box of Beaded Bracelets
    and Earrings—*New!***
**The Little Box of Beaded Necklaces
    and Earrings—*New!***
Miniature Punchneedle Embroidery
A Passion for Punchneedle
Scrapbooking Off the Page…
    and on the Wall
Sculpted Threads—*New!*

KNITTING & CROCHET
365 Knitting Stitches a Year:
    Perpetual Calendar
A to Z of Knitting—*New!*
Crochet from the Heart
Crocheted Pursenalities—*New!*
First Crochet
First Knits
Fun and Funky Crochet
Funky Chunky Knitted Accessories
Handknit Style II
The Knitter's Book of Finishing
    Techniques
Knitting with Gigi—*New!*
The Little Box of Crochet for Baby—*New!*
The Little Box of Knitted Throws
Modern Classics
More Sensational Knitted Socks—*New!*
Pursenalities
Top Down Sweaters—*New!*
Wrapped in Comfort—*New!*
The Yarn Stash Workbook

Our books are available at bookstores and your favorite craft, fabric,
and yarn retailers. If you don't see the title you're looking for,
visit us at **www.martingale-pub.com** or contact us at:

1-800-426-3126

International: 1-425-483-3313 • Fax: 1-425-486-7596 • Email: info@martingale-pub.com

3/07